THE POEMS OF CATULLUS

The Roman poet Catullus is one of the most popular and frequently studied ancient authors. His poems were written just over two thousand years ago during the chaotic but culturally vibrant final decades of the Republic and deal with themes of passion and grief, friendship and enmity, politics, literature and myth. This new translation, the product of a collaborative effort between a classicist and a poet, allows modern readers to experience his poems rather as his ancient Roman audience did. The poems are presented as contemporary and concise with a new energy and pace that both enhance Catullus' appeal for non-specialists and challenge specialists to consider his work from a fresh perspective. Extensive notes are provided, as well as an introduction which takes account of modern poetics and popular culture. The translation will appeal not only to classicists but also to lovers of literature in general and poetry in particular.

JEANNINE DIDDLE UZZI is Associate Professor of Classics at the University of Southern Maine. She is the author of *Children in the Visual Arts of Imperial Rome* (Cambridge, 2005). Other publications include 'The power of parenthood: women and children in official Roman art' in *Constructions of Childhood in Ancient Greece and Italy* (2007) and 'The age of consent: children and sexuality in ancient Greece and Rome' in *The Archaeology of Children: Interdisciplinary Approaches* (2015).

JEFFREY THOMSON is Professor of Creative Writing at the University of Maine, Farmington. He is the author of four books of poems, including *Birdwatching in Wartime*, winner of both the 2010 Maine Book Award and the 2011 ASLE Award in Environmental Creative Writing, and *Renovation*. In 2012 he was the Fulbright Distinguished Scholar in Creative Writing at the Seamus Heaney Poetry Centre at Queen's University Belfast and in 2015 he will be the Hodgson Trust-John Carter Brown Fellow at Brown University and the C. V. Starr Center for the Study of the American Experience at Washington College.

THE POEMS
OF
CATULLUS

AN ANNOTATED TRANSLATION

TRANSLATED BY

Jeannine Diddle Uzzi
Jeffrey Thomson

INTRODUCTION AND NOTES BY

Jeannine Diddle Uzzi

CAMBRIDGE
UNIVERSITY PRESS

CAMBRIDGE
UNIVERSITY PRESS

University Printing House, Cambridge CB2 8BS, United Kingdom

Cambridge University Press is part of the University of Cambridge.

It furthers the University's mission by disseminating knowledge in the pursuit of education, learning and research at the highest international levels of excellence.

www.cambridge.org
Information on this title: www.cambridge.org/9781107682139

First published 2015

Printed in the United States of America by Sheridan Books, Inc.

A catalogue record for this publication is available from the British Library

Library of Congress Cataloguing in Publication data
Catullus, Gaius Valerius.
[Works. English]
The Poems of Catullus : an annotated translation / Catullus ; Jeffrey Thomson and Jeannine Diddle Uzzi.
pages   cm
Translated from the Latin.
ISBN 978-1-107-02855-5 (hardback)
1. Catullus, Gaius Valerius – Translations into English.   I. Thomson, Jeffrey.
II. Uzzi, Jeannine Diddle, 1971–   III. Title.
PA6275.E5T47   2015
874′.01–dc23
2014048727

ISBN 978-1-107-02855-5 Hardback
ISBN 978-1-107-68213-9 Paperback

discipulis meis carissimis

– JDU

for Jennifer

– JT

Contents

Acknowledgments

We wish to thank all those who read these translations in their early stages and offered feedback of any sort: Peter Aicher, Eve Raimon, Dana Burgess, Stanley Lombardo, Amy Richlin, and Paul Allen Miller in addition to Michael Sharp and our Cambridge readers. We would also like to thank the University of Southern Maine and the University of Maine Farmington for the support that allowed us to begin this project. We would like to thank Whitman College for bringing us together and the Maine Classical Association. So many other people helped and supported us during this time: Jennifer Eriksen, Christian Barter, Kenny Morell, Heather Sawyer, and Wes McNair. It is also incumbent upon us to thank the many students who witnessed and vetted multiple versions of these translations including Robert Ballard, Emily Boutin, Katie Collins, Matthew Carter, Zachary Dickie, Brittany Goldych, Natasha Hayes, Anthony King, Hoda Mohammed, Casey Moore, Matthew Rodney, Lawrence Stevenson, Katie White, and Christopher Witham. Finally we would like to thank our mothers, Laura Diddle and Barbara Thomson, who taught us to love reading and poetry, although we are afraid they had no idea where their inspiration would finally lead!

Jeannine Diddle Uzzi and Jeffrey Thomson

Introduction

TRANSLATION AND THE CORPUS

1 Dedication

> To whom do I give my witty little book,
> newly buffed and pressed?
> To you, Cornelius: your singular audacity
> consigned to three sheets the history of the world –
> pithy but damned belabored.
> You always thought my little nothings something,
> so take this book, whatever sort it is,
> and, dear Muse, let it last.

When I began teaching I never imagined I would show Kevin Smith's *Clerks* in class. Don't get me wrong: I love the film, a 1994 comedy about a day in the life of two convenience store clerks in New Jersey, but it's not an obvious sell as classics, nor does its content lend itself to easy endorsement in the classroom. Nevertheless, I found myself pressing "play" in a big Roman civilization lecture and giving over to Jay and Silent Bob the ostensible *scaenae frons* (Roman stage) of my class. For this I have Amy Richlin to thank. In the introduction to her translation of Plautus' *Persa* (a play she titles *Iran Man*), Richlin claims that the films and comic books of Kevin Smith provide "a really excellent current parallel" (111) for the type of humor found in Plautus and, one might argue, Roman comedy in general. *Clerks* presents a world in which working-class youths run amuck while literally minding the shop. The perennial absence of an authority figure allows a cast of over-the-top slackers to engage in a particularly vulgar and subversive yet also literate and political brand of hilarity, the very brand one finds in the comic works of Plautus and Terence. While many classicists attempt to draw connections between the ancient and modern worlds, Richlin endeavors to translate the experience of being Roman, suggesting a way for modern audiences to encounter Roman comedy as the Romans might have. Watching *Clerks*, along with reading *Iran Man*, of course, we might approximate in a meaningful way what it was like to sit as a Roman in the audience of a comedy.

The desire to approximate the experience of the ancient audience for the modern is precisely what inspired this translation. Most modern translations of Catullus tend toward the literal, and even Charles Martin's translation, by many accounts the best English language translation of Catullus to date, follows Catullus' line breaks as if English-speaking readers had somehow internalized the Latin original. This approach to translation may have been good for students of Latin, but it has prevented Catullus from gaining the widespread appeal of poets like Homer, Sappho, and Vergil. Catullus' style is uncannily modern, his concerns timeless; in fact, as Martin himself notes, Catullus is probably the only classical poet to have had significant influence on modern English poetry.[1] In recent history, however, Catullus has been approached as a poet tied tightly to his historical context, ancient Rome of the late Republic, and useful primarily to students of Latin and classics.

Fortunately, one need not study classics to appreciate Catullus. Catullus is a poet of tragedy, a poet of wit, a poet of desire, and a poet whose voice cuts to the quick of human experience. Catullus' corpus runs its reader through the wringer of human emotion, from passion and humor to grief and loathing. The corpus is conscious of its literary and mythological roots, not to mention its own literarity; it presents language as inherently insufficient to its task and social norms as human constructions. Most of all, it recognizes the beautiful pain of

---

[1] Charles Martin, *The Poems of Catullus* (Johns Hopkins University Press, 1989): xxii. Martin credits Ezra Pound (1885–1972) with the "discovery" of Catullus for the modern world.

erotic desire as an essential condition of humanity, and it celebrates the unique ability of poetry to express that desire.

Catullus' dedicatory poem, translated above, is itself an excellent introduction to the corpus. In it the speaker describes his poetry, his "little book" (*libellum*), with three adjectives: *lepidum, novum,* and *expolitum* (properly, *expolitum* is a perfect passive participle, a verbal adjective meaning "having been polished"). He also calls his poems "trifles" or "nothings" (*nugas*) and claims at the end of the poem not to know what sort of little book he has created. Here Catullus is being coy, and obviously so; not only does Catullus know precisely what sort of book he has written, but he deliberately contrasts his book with the laborious (*laboriosis*) history of the world written by his dedicatee, Cornelius Nepos, a well-known Roman historian and biographer.

The first adjective, *lepidum,* can simply mean "pleasant," but it can also deliver a subtext of intellectual elitism. With this single adjective Catullus calls his poems pleasant or lovely but also urbane, elegant, learned, and charming. In the first poem we translate *lepidum* as "witty." While Roman wit could be charming and elegant, it could also be penetrating, aggressive, and cutting, and there is a good deal of this sort of wit in the Catullan corpus. While *lepidum* does not generally refer to a mordant type of humor, *lepidum* can mean facetious – almost sarcastic – as well as "so-nice-as-to-be-effeminate." In English, "wit" probably casts the widest net as a reference for a learned brand of oft-satirical humor whose insightfulness can be both eloquent and trenchant.

Novum seems easy enough, meaning very simply "new" and giving us the root for "novel" in English, but *novum* can also mean unique, contemporary, and fresh. The Roman orator Cicero makes reference to Catullus and his peer group of "new poets" at Rome using both the Latin *poetae novi* ("the new poets") and the Greek *neoteroi* (neoterics, literally "the younger ones").[2] The Romans, always in a love-hate relationship with

[2] See Cicero's *Orator* (161) and *Tusculan Disputations* (3.45). See also below, pp. 9 ff.

the Greeks, at once esteemed the literature of Greece and questioned the masculinity of the culture that produced it, so we ought to suspect that Cicero's use of a Greek descriptor is pejorative. Considering the fact that Cicero was a conservative senator and that his descriptions are probably insults, we might therefore think of *novum* as "non-traditional" or "irreverent," perhaps even "disrespectful." In "Dedication" (1) we hold *novum* until line two, making it there the simple adverb "newly," which has a web of meaning comprising synonyms like "freshly," "recently," and "again."

Finally we reach *expolitum*, arguably the most important of the three adjectives but also the most difficult since Catullus provides a tangible ancient context for it: he explains that his book is *expolitum*, literally "polished," by the very specific means of dry pumice (*arida pumice*). This description feels more technical than we, as modern readers, might like. If Catullus' poetry is so fresh and elegant, so *novum* and *lepidum*, why is he talking about pumice, even if it was used to smooth the end of a papyrus roll or erase mistakes on the page? If we appreciate the contrast between something that is highly polished and therefore smooth, slick, maybe even shiny, and a rough stone like pumice, we might get the joke, and if we were Roman, we would also know that pumice was used as a depilatory, and we might smile at the thought of a man's poetry being compared to a soft, smooth leg. Again, being Roman, and especially in light of the fact that *lepidum* can mean something close to "effeminate," we might also notice that Catullus is having fun here with gender, and we might even wonder whether the poet's body was as carefully plucked as his poetry.

As if we haven't pushed this term far enough, we can go a bit further to read *expolitum* as a reflection of the fact that Catullus' poetry is highly constructed and painstakingly crafted. While these descriptions are not unique to Catullus, his poetry navigates four significant obstacles modern poets can fairly easily avoid. First, Catullus inherited from his predecessors a complex system of metrics and in his fairly brief corpus employed more than ten different meters. At the same time,

Catullus wrote in an inflected language whose grammar and syntax are much more complex than those of English. Third, Catullus constructed a vocabulary unique to his corpus, even coining words like *basiationes*, which we translate as "kissings" in "Kissings of You" (7) but which literally is something equivalent to "kissifications." Finally, Catullus followed in the tradition of Callimachus, the Hellenistic poet who prized erudition second only to concision and is famous for having said that "a big book is a big evil."[3] Catullus' use of the diminutive *libellum* ("little book") to refer to his text in "Dedication" can certainly be read as an example of Catullus' special brand of self-deprecation, but it is also an apt description of his corpus, which comprises relatively few poems, many of which are themselves only a few lines long. Therefore, while in "Dedication" we translate *expolitum* with *novum* in order to describe Catullus' witty little book as "newly buffed," in my approach to translation I take *expolitum* so far as to mean concise.

Catullus' dedicatory poem provides not only an excellent introduction to the corpus but also an imperative for translation. Our English version of Catullus must be current and contemporary; it must be fresh, elegant, and witty, and it must appeal to a literary audience. Finally, it must be smooth, effortless, concise, and well-crafted. In his provocative essay "The Task of the Translator,"[4] Walter Benjamin (1892–1940) compares translation to art restoration:

> Fragments of a vessel which are to be glued together must match one another in the smallest details, although they need not be like one

---

[3] This quote is recorded by Athenaeus, ii.72a. Catullus pays homage to Callimachus in "Kissings of You" when he refers to Cyrene and "the sacred tomb of old Battus." Cyrene was the birthplace of the Hellenistic poet Callimachus and Battus the legendary ancestor of that poet. In "Like an Apple" (65) and "Archery" (116), Catullus calls Callimachus *Battiades*, "descended from Battus."

[4] From Walter Benjamin, *Illuminations* (Schocken Books, 1968, reprinted by Random House, 2007), translated by Harry Zohn. In the original German title of his essay, "*Die Aufgabe des Übersetzers*," *Aufgabe*, translated "task" by Zohn, can also mean "abandonment" or "surrender," leading some to read the essay as a prohibition against translation altogether. *Aufgabe*, however, weaves a fairly broad web of meaning and can be translated "duty," "problem," "task," and "lesson" in addition to "giving up," "abandonment," and "surrender." I prefer to think of Benjamin's article as "The Yielding of the Translator" in order to make clear Benjamin's assertion that the translator must yield, must give up the impulse toward literal reproduction of meaning.

> another. In the same way a translation, instead of resembling the meaning of the original, must lovingly and in detail incorporate the original's mode of signification, thus making both the original and the translation recognizable as fragments of a greater language, just as fragments are part of a vessel (Ibid., 78).

Having spent the bulk of my career studying Roman historical relief, I find Benjamin's analogy of the fragmented vessel particularly appealing: Benjamin has a great deal to offer the translator struggling to find a coherent voice across such great divides of time, space, and culture as separate us from Catullus. "[A]s regards the meaning," Benjamin says, "the language of translation can – in fact, must – let itself go, so that it gives voice to the *intentio* of the original not as reproduction but as harmony, as a supplement to the language in which it expresses itself, as its own kind of *intentio*" (Ibid., 79). While we do not present here a literal translation of Catullus' Latin, neither is this collection "adapted from" or "inspired by" Catullus. We have tried to capture in English the spirit and essence, the *intentio*, of each of Catullus' poems, allowing the original content, form, and language to inspire our native language, and approximating for a modern audience the experience of reading Catullus as a Roman might have. If we have failed, Benjamin has provided us an apology of sorts: "[N]o case for literalness can be based on a desire to retain the meaning. Meaning is served far better – and literature and language far worse – by the unrestrained license of bad translators" (Ibid., 78).

Ancient authors did not give titles to individual short poems. The titles we have added are neither enigmatic nor distinct from the poems themselves: they are crucial elements of the translations, sometimes taken from Latin words or lines we do not address in the body of a poem. Our titles both set the stage for the poems and complement and support the lines they introduce. Catullus' poems are presented here in their transmitted order; however, this is not necessarily the order in which the poet arranged them. The manuscript tradition of Catullus is rife with uncertainty; as Micaela Janan so elegantly notes, "Catullus is a poet about whom everything is difficult".[5] We have therefore chosen to present the poems in the order in which they are now generally published, organized by metrics rather than by narrative or theme.

CATULLUS IN CONTEXT

Historical

While one need not study classics to appreciate Catullus, many readers will find historical context for the poetry helpful. Scholarly consensus is that Catullus lived probably between 84 and 54 BC. We know very little about the specifics of the poet's life, but it is clear from his poetry that Catullus was wealthy and educated, the product of a privileged environment. Catullus was born in Verona, which was in his time part of the province of Cisalpine Gaul (Gaul On-the-Near-Side-of-the-Alps), to a family that was apparently well connected at Rome and tied somehow to Julius Caesar. At some point in his early adulthood Catullus moved to Rome, and scholars generally agree that Catullus spent time in Bithynia, a Roman province in what is now northern Turkey, where he served in some official capacity under the governor C. Memmius.[6]

During Catullus' brief lifetime, Rome was a city in turmoil.[7] Suffice it to say here that Catullus was a toddler during the dictatorship and

[5] Micaela Janan, *"When the Lamp is Shattered": Desire and Narrative in Catullus* (Southern Illinois University Press, 1994): ix. Those interested in the manuscript tradition of Catullus or the order of the poems should consult L. D. Reynolds and N. G. Wilson, *Scribes and Scholars* (Oxford University Press, 1991) and Marilyn Skinner, *Catullus' Passer* (Ayer, 1992) as excellent starting points. Peter Green's introduction to his *The Poems of Catullus: A Bilingual Edition* (University of California Press, 2005) provides a brief overview of the transmission and reception of the Catullan corpus.

[6] Mining literary texts for biographical information about their authors is generally suspect; however, "The Whore" (10) and "Not For Profit" (28) present fairly intimate knowledge of the political situation in Bithynia under Memmius.

[7] Much has been written about the end of the Roman Republic and the transitional period from Republic to Empire. I like T. P. Wiseman's slim volume *Roman Political Life* (University of Exeter Press, 1985), which includes a timeline of events from the Social War of 90 BC to the end of the Julio-Claudian dynasty in 69 AD, and Ronald Syme's tremendous tome *The Roman Revolution*, of which a revised edition of the 1951 original was offered by Oxford University Press in 2002. I also recommend HBO's *Rome* to anyone interested in a provocative introduction to the period – classicists generally love the series. Be aware, however, that by the end of the first season Catullus

7

proscriptions of Sulla, a young man during the so-called Catilinarian conspiracy and the First Triumvirate of Pompey, Crassus, and Caesar, and an adult when Julius Caesar became consul and Cicero was exiled from Rome. Just five years after Catullus' death, assuming that he indeed died in 54 BC, Caesar crossed the Rubicon into Rome, a move that resulted in years of civil war between Caesar and Pompey and, one could argue, Caesar's eventual assassination, not to mention the end of the Roman Republic. The years in which Catullus lived were bleak ones for Rome, years of transition and strife, years in which loyalties changed with the tides and uncertainty reigned. It was a troubled social and political context that birthed Catullus, and we find residue of this fact in his poetry.

Literary

It will come as no surprise that these turbulent times appear to have engendered literary innovation. We in the modern West seem to believe that great hardship produces great art. Perhaps this is true; perhaps it was true for Catullus; perhaps with the political uncertainty of Catullus' time came a certain freedom from convention. Whatever the reason, there is good evidence that Catullus was part of a new literary coterie, a circle of poets in Rome whom Cicero called "neoteric"[8]. Cicero's use of the Greek here calls to mind Alexandria and the Hellenistic poets, of whom Callimachus is the most well known and most influential.

Prior to the first century BC very little lyric poetry was written in Latin.[9] Early Roman poetry was almost entirely epic or dramatic, although the Romans also wrote satire, and Catullus is probably reacting and responding in his corpus to all these poetic forms. Catullus also makes obvious his

---

would already have died; Julius Caesar was assassinated ten years *after* Catullus' death, assuming again that Catullus died in 54 BC.

[8] See n. 2 above.

[9] Lyric poetry meant something different to the Romans than it does to modern readers of English. Technically speaking, Catullus did not confine himself to lyric meters; however, Catullus is received by modern English readers as a writer of Latin lyric – poetry written often from a personal perspective, often expressing subjective thoughts and/or feelings.

Greek literary roots via invocations of and allusions to Sappho and Callimachus. Apart from Cicero's label, Catullus' own poetry is the best extant evidence for a new poetic movement at Rome, and Catullus does offer hints that some sort of self-conscious literary innovation was, in fact, happening in first-century BC Rome. In his poetry Catullus mentions favorably a number of other poets likely to have been members of his literary circle: C. Licinius Calvus Macer, perhaps the Licinius of "Erotica" (50), the Caecilius of "Unfinished" (35), and Gaius Cinna,[10] the Cinna of "Cinna's Epic Reduction" (95ab).[11] Catullus draws clear distinctions between his poetry and the work of other authors including his dedicatee, Cornelius Nepos, in "Dedication," the poet Volusius in "Into the Fire" (36), and other "appalling" poets (Caesius, Aquinus, Suffenus) in "The Gift" (14). The distinctions Catullus makes between the works of these poets and those of his own literary circle are given depth in "Cinna's Epic Reduction," where Catullus praises the painstakingly polished literary work of Cinna, contrasting with it both the bombastic works of Hortensius (Q. Hortensius Hortalus) and Antimachus (of Colophon)[12] as well as the "crap" poetry (*cacata carta* in "Into the Fire") written by Volusius:

95ab Cinna's Epic Reduction[13]

After nine harvests, nine winters' labor,
Cinna has finally birthed his "Zmyrna."
Hortensius, meanwhile, spewed
half a million lines ...
"Zmyrna's" deep fame will outlast generations,
outspread the river it celebrates,
while Volusius' pages languish,

---

[10] Gaius Cinna may be the same Cinna as C. Helvius Cinna, tribune of 44 BC.

[11] The Cato of "Laughable" (56) may also fit this bill, but the case is far from clear.

[12] In the Hellenistic period the poet Callimachus had similarly criticized the *Lyde* of Antimachus of Colophon for being overly wordy.

[13] Ellipses in our translations indicate lines or fragments of lines of the Latin originals lost in transmission.

damp wrapping for mackerel
in the shallows of the Po ...
... the annals of my heart are small ...
let the horde have tumid Antimachus.

Catullus' poetry gives us a feel for his literary sensibilities and probably does illuminate the aesthetic of his literary circle. Catullus was an innovator; he was highly educated, yet he wrote (and perhaps also lived) outside the social mainstream. He probably died young, and what little he wrote was intended for an elite audience.

POETICS

We might profitably compare Catullus and his fellow poets with Percy Bysshe Shelley's literary circle of the early nineteenth century or with the New York Beat poets, literary innovators and social deviants who represent a movement characterized by erudition and collaboration. Perhaps there is an even more provocative possibility, or, to borrow Amy Richlin's phrase, a "really excellent current parallel" for Catullus: I suggest Eminem.[14] Like Catullus in "Cinna's Epic Reduction," Eminem writes and raps about creating and performing within an artistic community. And like Catullus, Eminem critiques his peers in a sometimes dichotomous combination of competition and collaboration. In "Message to My Love" (11) and "Persona" (16) Catullus addresses the same two men, Furius and Aurelius. "Message to My Love" asks the pair to deliver a message to Lesbia, calling Furius and Aurelius friends or companions (*comites*), but "Persona," translated below, berates the pair for misunderstanding the relationship between poet and poetry, threatening them with

---

[14] I am not the first to imagine Eminem as a parallel for Catullus. In a *Jacket Magazine* review of Peter Green's Catullus translations, Tim Keane calls "Her Husband" (83) "invective worthy of Eminem" (*Jacket* 34, October 2007: *Jacket* is a free, online literary magazine). There is also a brief reference to Catullus and Eminem on *Bootstrap News* (bootstrapproductions.blogspot.com) for June 23, 2008. While the comparison is far from mainstream, there is fairly widespread acknowledgment of Eminem's talent as a poet, and his fans include the late Nobel laureate Seamus Heaney (Adam Bradley and Andrew Dubois, *The Anthology of Rap*, (Yale University Press, 2010): 611).

sexual assault. The violence of these verses might shock the modern reader, but such violence was not uncommon in Latin poetry, and Catullus probably draws here from Greek and Roman literary precedents including comedy.

16 Persona

> I'll fuck you in the mouth and ass,
> Furius and Aurelius, you pair of fags.
> You think I'm like my lines,
> a little too soft, too flamboyant?
> Sure, a man should control himself
> but not necessarily his verses,
> which have only wit and charm
> if they are sexy and supple
> and can get a rise
> not just from boys but from hairy old men
> whose dicks are dull and stuck.
> You think I'm a pussy
> when you read my "thousand kisses"?
> I'll fuck you in the mouth and ass!

While the historical identification of characters in a literary text is necessarily tenuous, evidence suggests that Furius is probably the poet Marcus Furius Bibaculus, to whom the historian/biographer Suetonius ascribes two surviving epigrams.[15] If so, Catullus presents his speaker and Furius in a complex relationship we might characterize on the one hand as intimate or collaborative and on the other hand as fraught and agonistic. Furius is Catullus' respected peer when it suits him in "Message to My Love", and a misguided competitor when it doesn't

---

[15] We can say nothing about the identity of Aurelius, who is mentioned in "Message to My Love" (11), "This One Boy" (15), "Persona" (16), and "This One Boy II" (21). Furius is also mentioned in "Dry and Crisp" (23) and "Encumbered" (26), the latter of which is a poem similar to that recorded by Suetonius and attributed to M. Furius Bibaculus – both are based on puns (see Suetonius, *De Grammaticis* 11, Kenneth Quinn, *Catullus: The Poems* (St. Martin's Press, 1973): 169, and Julia W. Loomis "M. Furius Bibaculus and Catullus," *Classical World* 63.4 (1969): 112–114).

in "Persona." Likewise, Eminem has collaborated with fellow rapper Dr. Dre on songs from "What's the Difference" (Dr. Dre, *2001*) to "I Need a Doctor" (Dr. Dre, single released February, 2011), but Eminem also engages in rhetorical competition with the rapper, claiming in "Criminal" (Eminem, *The Marshall Mathers LP*) to hold Dre captive: "that's Dre with an AK to his face." We see in Eminem's construction of his relationship with Dr. Dre the sort of relationship Catullus' corpus presents between Catullus and Furius.

While Catullus and Eminem both define their work and their personae within and against an artistic peer group, the similarities between them go far beyond the communal: there is something specifically Catullan in Eminem. Both Catullus and Eminem present themselves as outsiders (albeit elite ones) engaged in non-normative activity even within their artistic circles. Eminem is conscious of being one of the few successful white rappers: "I don't do black music, I don't do white music, I make fight music" ("Who Knew," *The Marshall Mathers LP*). And as the artist 50 Cent has noted, "The best rapper is a white man" (Bradley and Dubois 611).[16] The Steve Berman Skit on *The Marshall Mathers LP* futher illuminates Eminem's outsider status. In the skit, Berman chides Eminem, "Do you know why Dre's album was so successful? He's rapping about big screen TVs, blunts, 40s, and bitches. You're rapping about homosexuals and Vicodin."

Catullus' persona is concerned not with race but with gender, presenting a masculine identity questionable within Roman norms. In fact, in "Message to My Love," Catullus' speaker goes so far as to figuratively castrate himself, saying that Lesbia has "clipped our love/ like a bloom on the field's edge,/cut short by a passing plow."[17] Likewise, in "It's Over" (8), Catullus' speaker urges himself again and again to "be a man,"

---

[16] Ross McCammon, "50 Cent: What I've Learned," Esquire, January 2010, www.esquire.com/features/what-ive-learned/new-50-cent-interview-0110 (as quoted in Bradley and Dubois, *Anthology* 807fn.20).

[17] This is not the only poem in which the speaker's castration is implied. See more on castration below, pp. 24 ff.

to "stop embarrassing [him]self." "Sappho's Poem/Get a Job" (51) cuts to the core of the speaker's improper masculinity in its identification of Catullus as a man of leisure: the speaker is presented without proper male occupation to keep him from his poetry. In Latin, leisure is *otium*, its etymological and conceptual opposite *negotium*. That is, Latin makes explicit the fact that business is the negation of leisure: *ne–[g]otium*. Catullus also explores the problem of leisure in "The Whore" (10), where the speaker is found at leisure (*otiosum*: "I had the time") in the Forum, the primary locus of Roman business.

In addition, Eminem and Catullus both dissociate themselves as individuals from their artistic products, claiming not to enact or endorse things they write or say. In "Criminal," Eminem muses, "A lot of people ask me stupid fuckin' questions, a lot of people think that what I say on record or what I talk about on a record, that I actually do in real life or that I believe in it, or if I say that I wanna kill somebody that I'm actually gonna do it or I believe in it, well, shit, if you believe that, then I'll kill you." The final lines of the violently misogynistic "Kill You" (*The Marshall Mathers LP*) claim, "Ha ha, I'm just playin' ladies, you know I love you." Catullus dissociates his own *mores* from the *mores* of his poetry in "Persona," asking, "You think I'm like my verses,/a little too soft, too flamboyant?/Sure, a man should control himself,/but not necessarily his verses ... You think I'm a pussy ...?/I'll fuck you in the mouth and ass." With a dark but humorous irony that is certainly intentional, Eminem and Catullus both answer the ostensible accusations against them by threatening to perform the very behaviors they deny. Eminem threatens to kill in "Criminal," while in "Persona" Catullus threatens behavior that is neither controlled nor chaste: the oral and anal rape of his addressees.

Finally, there are myriad similarities between the artistic corpora of Catullus and Eminem. As I finish editing this essay, in his latest single "The Monster," featuring Rihanna, on *The Marshall Mathers LP 2*, Eminem says, "Well, I ain't much of a poet," echoing the mock self-deprecation of Catullus' "Dedication". Both Catullus and Eminem employ aggressive, hyper-masculine rhetoric characterized by a type of homophobia that borders on and in some cases allows for homoeroticism, both artists assert their masculine identities in part through misogynistic language, and both artists refer to their personae in the third person. Eminem's lyrics are driven by an intense aggression, an aggression Catullus can match dig for dig, and both artists create a shocking type of satire stuck somewhere between hilarious and horrifying. Catullus and Eminem also manipulate language in seemingly effortless rivers of narrative and invective, coining words and compiling vocabularies through which they visit and revisit themes central to their artistic products. In short, both artists present a corpus of work that can and should be read and reread backwards and forwards, inside and out.[18]

Our comparison, of course, is imperfect. Eminem is by no means a modern Catullus, but his music offers a modern audience a compelling parallel for certain aspects of Catullus' voice and poetry, particularly where Catullus' artistic community and the masculine identity of his speaker are concerned. If we extend the comparison to include artists like Jay Z and Tupac (2Pac), we find that rap as a genre offers a number of additional parallels for Catullus' poetry. Jay Z's presentation of himself as the ruler, the king, the guy "on top" is something like Catullus' presentation of himself as the poetic master; Catullus may be more subtle or coy, but his message is similar. And like Catullus' corpus, rap is not all bravado and invective but is woven with tragedy and desire. Rap presents impossible situations in which characters in the narrative find themselves unable to escape death, pain, and loss just as Catullus is unable to escape the pain of losing Lesbia or his brother or the insult of being betrayed or rejected. The importance of such themes in rap is evident in a debate over the attribution of the following lyrics: "get zipped up in plastic, when it happens, that's it." I know the

---

[18] This is precisely the approach to reading lyric poetry that Paul Allen Miller recommends in his *Lyric Texts and Lyric Consciousness* (Routledge, 1994).

line from Jay Z's "Takeover," but fans online claim that Jay Z took it from a similar line written by Dr. Dre. Important here is not the attribution but the debate itself, which indicates that this sort of cold acknowledgment of mortality is so common in rap that it's hard to know who coined which lines, even for die-hard fans.

In "U Don't Know" on *The Blueprint*, Jay-Z paints a tragic picture akin to that offered by David Simon's HBO series *The Wire*: "They say that we are prone to violence, but it's home sweet home where personalities clash and chrome meets chrome … welcome to Hell." Tupac's final album *Me Against the World* is itself a meditation on death and loss including the touching homage "Dear Mama" and a number of songs presenting the rapper as unable to face the reality of the situation in which he portrays himself. "Young Niggaz" is in part a cautionary tale for the next generation; "Death Around the Corner" treats the terror of facing one's own mortality, and "Lord Knows" includes the following lyrics: "I smoke a blunt to take the pain out, if I wasn't high I'd probably try to blow my brains out … they shoulda killed me as a baby … they wanna see me in my casket … I'm losing hope." In these songs we hear some of the pain and frustration of "It's Over" (8), "The Ugly Truth" (73), "Exhaustion" (75), and "Ave atque vale" (101).[19] Again, the comparison is imperfect: we may never find a rap equivalent for Catullus' wedding poems, but if we begin with Eminem and broaden our thinking to include Eminem's artistic peers, we may find that rap as a genre offers a great deal of food for thought where Catullus' corpus is concerned and perhaps even a worthwhile modern analogue for Catullus' poetry.

LESBIA AND OTHER EROTICA

The Catullan corpus, though small, is far-reaching in the subjects and themes it explores and the poetic styles it employs. Catullus writes

---

[19] My favorite recent example of the picture of frustration and futility rap can present is 50 Cent's "My Life" feat. Eminem and Adam Levine (2012), which itself alludes to those disputed lyrics "get zipped up in plastic."

about love affairs and friends, poets and politicians, life in Rome and abroad; he writes long poems on familiar episodes from classical mythology, wedding hymns, invective, satire, and poems about intimate topics like the death of his brother or his desire for a boy or youth called Juventius. In a corpus of fewer than 120 poems, Catullus employs more than ten different meters including hendecasyllabics (11-syllable lines), Sapphic stanzas, dactylic hexameters (the meter of epic poetry), and elegiac couplets. Within this diverse corpus, however, we find one coherent narrative thread known as the Lesbia cycle, those poems related to a love affair between the male speaker of the corpus and a female figure known only as Lesbia. The poems of the Lesbia cycle, sprinkled throughout the corpus, address Catullus' poetic project, define Catullus' voice, and offer an elegant case study from which to approach the corpus as a whole.[20]

Who was Lesbia? On this question much ink has been spilled, most of which flows in the wrong direction if one is interested in poetry per se. The best answer is that Lesbia is the name Catullus gives to the primary love interest of his male speaker. She is the female character who figures largest in Catullus' corpus, and Catullus provides her with a strong and compelling personality, if not voice. Classicists have suggested that the poet used the name Lesbia as a pseudonym for a mistress, perhaps Clodia Metelli, sister of Publius Clodius Pulcher and wife of Quintus Metellus Celer, the woman whom Cicero's *pro Caelio* impugns. The best evidence for this argument is found in Catullus' poem "Her Brother" (79), which begins *Lesbius est pulcher*, perhaps associating Lesbia with the Pulcher family. For those interested, the sourcebook on Clodia by Julia

---

[20] The boundaries of the Lesbia cycle are themselves blurry: should the cycle include only poems that name Lesbia? How can we be certain that any single poem without the name Lesbia belongs to the cycle? Can we define a vocabulary unique to the Lesbia cycle (including *puella*, *deliciae*, and *passer*, for instance)? My philosophy is inclusive: in addition to all poems that name Lesbia or make obvious reference to her, I consider in this category all poems even marginally or arguably related to Lesbia as well as poems that help us understand the Lesbia cycle because of the vocabulary or tropes they employ.

Dyson Hejduk (*Clodia: A Sourcebook.* University of Oklahoma Press, 2008) explores this possibility in copious detail, concluding, as do most studies, that Lesbia "was" Clodia. Readers may also enjoy Marilyn Skinner's more recent *Clodia Metelli: The Tribune's Sister* (Oxford University Press, 2011), which while skirting the question of whether Catullus loved a "flesh-and-blood Clodia" also claims that Catullus is remembered at least in part for "what he made of Cicero's Clodia" (Skinner, *Clodia Metelli,* 149), necessarily affirming a Lesbia–Clodia connection.

It is not my intention to weigh in on the discussion or to recount it here; suffice it to say that the identification of an historical Lesbia is unnecessary for understanding Catullus' poetic project. While the identity of Catullus' lover may have been of significant interest to his friends and fellow poets, it is of little use to the modern reader or, in fact, to any reader without intimate knowledge of the poet's life, on whom all specific, personal references are lost and for whom the corpus stands independent from its author. Catullus may indeed have had a love affair with Clodia Metelli, but the Lesbia of his corpus is necessarily a literary construct. While classicists have longed to find the *real* Lesbia, the *true* Lesbia, the *historical* Lesbia, Lesbia has been living all the while within the poetry that created her. Interest in an historical Lesbia has prevented readers from approaching Lesbia as she is best approached: a referent for Catullus' core poetic concerns.

The Lesbia cycle is most obviously an erotic narrative, perhaps the most compelling erotic narrative to survive from the ancient world. In it, Catullus illustrates for his audience the full arc of the troubled relationship between Lesbia and the Catullan speaker, from its blissful beginnings and perhaps naïve dream of commitment and contentment to a period of doubt and infidelity to the destructive fixation of the speaker on Lesbia, including his almost pathological inability to let her go, to his final resentment and loathing of the woman he can never possess. In the cycle Catullus paints a believable portrait of a passionate love affair that borders on obsession, reminding one of the Eminem–Rihanna collaboration "Love the Way You Lie" (Eminem, *Recovery*).

Catullus' brief "Odetamo" (85) captures with elegant simplicity the rich essence of the Lesbia cycle. The title of the poem is an elision of three Latin words, *odi et amo*, "I hate and I love," which, when spoken aloud in verse, create a single figurative verb of hating and loving, *odetamo*:

85 Odetamo

> I hate and I love.
> Perhaps you wonder why.
> I don't know, but I feel it, and I am crucified.

In these three lines, Catullus conflates the romantic sentiment of poems like "Time and Number" (5) and "Kissings of You" with the venom of "Message to My Love" and "That Lesbia" (58) and even the despair of "Exhaustion" and "Wind and Water" (70). The Lesbia cycle captures its audience in an erotic encounter that resounds with all the beauty, pain, and power of the most memorable stories of love and love lost. Indeed, the Lesbia cycle sets the stage for future erotic narratives in Latin and beyond.

The significance of the Lesbia cycle moves far beyond its own narrative, however, and the name Lesbia indicates that the cycle is every bit as much about poetry as it is about a relationship with any single female figure, real or imagined. Assuming the poet was in need of a pseudonym for a specific mistress, the field of names available to him was wide and Lesbia far from common. Catullus chose for his most significant female character the female form of the adjective that means "from Lesbos."[21] Were a modern poet to use such a name, readers would no doubt assume that he/she intended to allude to female homoeroticism. For Catullus' audience, however, the name Lesbia invoked one person: Sappho, an archaic Greek poet, the first and most important

---

[21] The comic playwright Terence includes a character called Lesbia (a midwife from the island of Lesbos) in his play *Andria*.

female author known to us from Greece and a Lesbian in the geographical sense: Sappho hailed from the island of Lesbos.[22]

Whether Sappho herself did or did not engage in homoerotic activity (all evidence is to the affirmative, but from what little we know about female homoeroticism in the ancient world, it's clear that this question is much more interesting to us now than it was to anyone writing or creating art in Sappho's time), Sappho is arguably the single most important poetic predecessor of Catullus and certainly someone to whom Catullus considered himself in tremendous debt. "Sappho's Poem/Get a Job" is our translation of Catullus' poem 51, which was Catullus' translation of Sappho's poem 31 (*phainetai moi*). The name Lesbia, therefore, does refer to a specific historical figure but not necessarily and certainly not first to Clodia Metelli. With the name Lesbia Catullus pays homage to the poet Sappho and, by extension, the Greek poetic history that precedes him.

In "Translation and the corpus" above, I characterized Catullus as a poet of desire. I take the meaning of desire from the Greek root of the word erotic (*eros*), which refers not only to sexual desire but also to a sense of longing for something one lacks. In Plato's *Symposium* love is defined as a lack, as a desire to possess (*epithumein*) that which one does not have.[23] The relationship between the speaker of the corpus and the Lesbia he creates is certainly erotic, but it reflects not only the relationship between a lover and his beloved but also the relationship between a poet and his poetry, and a man and his identity.[24]

---

[22] Dillon and Garland suggest that the name Lesbia might also refer to the verbal form of the Greek root, *lesbiazein*, to perform oral sex (Matthew Dillon and Lynda Garland, *Ancient Rome: From the Early Republic to the Assassination of Julius Caesar* (Routledge, 2005): 372).

[23] *Symposium* 200A–B, see the translation by Alexander Nehamas and Paul Woodruff, *Symposium* (Hackett Publishing Company, 1989): 41. Diotima in the *Symposium* goes on to explain that, properly, "love is wanting to possess the good forever" (206A), but for our purposes, the important aspect of her definition is that, presumably, no human being could possess the good forever.

[24] I use "his" here pointedly since the Catullan corpus is so clearly concerned with issues of masculinity; however, it is certainly the case that any poet could be seen as having an erotic relationship with his/her poetry and/or identity.

In "Into the Fire" Catullus creates an intimate relationship between Lesbia and poetry via a pair of superlatives: the worst girlfriend and the worst poetry. Calling Lesbia the "worst girlfriend of all" immediately after his indictment of the "very worst poetry," the speaker characterizes Lesbia in the same terms as Volusius' offensive verses, tempting the reader to conflate Lesbia with verse: in Latin, the verses are *pessimi*, the girlfriend *pessima*.

36 Into the Fire

Shitty scraps of Volusius,
secure my love's vow:
to Venus and Cupid she swore —
provided I apologize,
stop brandishing my polished insults —
that she would consecrate to the limping god
a burnt offering:
the best of the very worst poetry.
She, the worst girlfriend of all,
thought she'd charm the gods with her sham —
now Aphrodite, Seafoam Goddess of Idalion
and Urion by-the-sea,
Ancon and stalky Knidos, Amathos and Golgi
and Dyrrachion, Ocean's pub,
reckon her debt as paid, if that's not base or coarse —
and you, shitty scraps, countrified crap
Volusius calls poetry, leap into the fire.

In the poem, the foul poetry secures Lesbia's vow that she will take the speaker back, provided he stop inveighing against her. That is, the worst poetry and the worst girlfriend are not only described in identical terms; in the poem's narrative, they are also in cahoots.

Lesbia is also conflated with poetry in "Atalanta" (2ab), in which the speaker wishes he could "relieve the pain of wanting her" (line 7).

2ab Atalanta

Bird, little toy of my love,
the one she teases and holds close,
provokes to nip and bite when the heat demands diversion,
distraction from desire to soothe the burning ache,
(at least that's how I see it):
if only I could play with you like that,
relieve the pain of wanting her ...

    ... this would be my golden apple
like the one that freed a nimble maiden
from a chastity belt so long bound tight.

The noun rendered here "pain" is the Latin *curas*, most simply "cares" in English. Other translators have called Catullus' *curas* "depression" (Green) and "passion" (Martin), but while *curas* in Latin can be the cares or anxieties induced by love, *curas* refers more generally to any objects of care as well as to the management or administration of one's responsibilities and affairs. *Curas* can refer in particular to writing or written works, like the ancient Greek *melete*, which in addition to "care" meant "pursuit," "practice," or "exercise," as in the practice of writing. While it is more common for later Latin to use *curas* to refer to writing – the usage is found especially in Tacitus – one can profitably read Lesbia in the Catullan corpus as "the practice of writing."

In fact, the corpus invites the reader to conflate poetics and erotics more generally. In line 6 of "Atalanta," the speaker wishes he could play with Lesbia's pet bird since he cannot play with Lesbia, and the verb he uses to indicate "play" (*ludere*) connotes, at least in part, erotic play. Catullus uses the same verb of playing in "Erotica" (50) to describe the poetic process in which his speaker and another poet, Licinius, are engaged. The verb used here is *lusimus*, a perfect form of the verb *ludere*. Like "Atalanta," "Erotica" creates slippage between erotic play and creative expression, sexual desire and poetic inspiration. It is impossible for the reader of "Erotica" to divorce the speaker's sexual desire from his desire to write poetry; the poem begins with poetic collaboration, which leads to erotic desire, the result of which is poetry: "I wrote this poem" (line 12):

50 Erotica

Yesterday, Licinius, when we played –
we both felt it –
making sweet verse,
flirting with beats back and forth,
harmonizing, warm with wine.
Singed by your wit, I left
unfastened, overcome:
no relief in food or sleep,
I knotted the sheets,
longing for sunrise and you.
Spent and sprawled, limp,
I wrote this poem:
be kind, darling, and beware,
lest Nemesis exact her price;
she's a holy terror: don't piss her off.

"Erotica"[25] sums up the relationship between desire and poetry in the Catullan corpus, reflecting a literary erotics in which *eros* and *logos* are conflated. Poetic composition is an erotic pursuit for the Catullan speaker, and in poems like "Into the Fire" and "Atalanta," Lesbia represents, at least in part, the artistic product Catullus pursues.

If Lesbia can be read as poetry, the object of the poet's erotic desire, then we ought to examine the speaker of the poems as a desiring subject. When we do, we find that the speaker explores and expresses deep concerns about his own gendered identity in the Lesbia cycle. A quick survey of how frequently the speaker talks to himself, refers to

---

[25] In light of our discussion of leisure above, it is worth noting that the first line of "Erotica" presents Catullus and Licinius as *otiosi* (at leisure).

himself in the third person, or uses first-person pronouns or possessive adjectives (I, me, my, mine) indicates that the Lesbia cycle has as much to say about its desiring subject as it does about the objects of his desire.

The final lines of "It's Over" read, "But you, Catullus ... be a man."[26] This command echoes the first line of the same poem in which the speaker says, "Catullus, you're pathetic." The speaker's problem in "It's Over" is not that Lesbia has abandoned him or that their relationship has ended; the problem is that the speaker's situation with respect to Lesbia threatens his masculinity:

8 It's Over

Catullus, you're pathetic.
Stop embarrassing yourself:
open your eyes.
You had your Golden Age,
prancing like a schoolgirl after that whore,
like no man ever did nor will again.
When she was game, you played everything
she'd allow –
you had your Golden Age.
Now she's unwilling and you're unmanned.
Don't pant after rejection, crave humiliation;
be strong; keep your head.
Goodbye, love; *now* Catullus is strong.
He won't ask, won't beg.
But you, you'll be wretched
when no one cares.
What's left for you?

---

[26] Of course, our translation is not literal. The final lines of the Latin poem literally say something like "Having been determined/fixed, be hard/persist!" And now the reader can see exactly why Benjamin urged translators to avoid the impulse toward literal translation! Other translators have said "keep your mind made up, hang tough!" (Green) and "You must hold out now, firmly!" (Martin).

> Who will want you? Who will think you're worth it?
> Who will you kiss? Who bite?
> But you, Catullus, come on: be a man.

If we look closely at the characterization of the male speaker in the Lesbia cycle, we shall discover why the speaker cannot end his affair with Lesbia, why he can't "be a man": Catullus' speaker is consistently portrayed as submissive, passive, and therefore, from the point of view of normative Roman culture, emasculated, playing what the Romans would have considered the female role. Catullus' male speaker cannot act – he must be acted upon.

Anyone familiar with Michel Foucault's analysis of ancient sexuality will recognize his influence on my reading of Catullus.[27] Speaking broadly, it is more useful to think of ancient sexuality in terms of agency or power than in terms of gender. A Roman male citizen was expected to play the role of the active sexual subject, the aggressor and penetrator, while women and those of lower status, often regardless of gender, were seen as sexual objects or recipients, the passive partners of male citizens. Throughout the Lesbia cycle, though, Catullus is rarely in control, and the poet goes so far as to castrate his male speaker not once but twice.

There are four poems in which the speaker presents himself as a woman or eunuch. In "Atalanta," the speaker likens himself to a woman struggling with the expectations of virginity, desperate to break free. In "Epyllion" (64), we see our speaker in the abandoned figure of Ariadne, where Theseus stands for Lesbia. And in "Wild Side" (63), the Catullan speaker can be found in the castrated figure of Attis, the "flower" of the youth, just as the speaker is compared to a flower and castrated ("clipped"/"cut short") in "Message to My Love". Ironically, in "Message to My Love" the castration follows the speaker's assertion of his own proper male aggression, in which he travels the outskirts of the

---

[27] See especially *The Use of Pleasure*, vol. 2 of Michel Foucault, *The History of Sexuality* (Vintage, 1990).

Roman world, "invading" and "penetrating" non-Romans. In "Wild Side," both in the Latin and in our translation, the pronoun used for the speaking subject of the poem changes from masculine to feminine following the castration.

There is one realm, however, in which the Catullan speaker is not powerless: language. Catullus may give Lesbia agency in his poetic narrative, but he keeps a stranglehold on her voice. In not one poem does Lesbia successfully speak for herself.[28] Catullus' speaker reports Lesbia's speech indirectly; he paraphrases and reinterprets Lesbia's speech; even what appear to be Lesbia's clearest statements of fact (reported, of course, by the speaker) eventually prove false, untrustworthy, or unknowable. Jacques Lacan[29] would say that Lesbia's speech is the speech of the feminine.[30] What exactly does this mean? Without delving too deeply into Lacanian psychoanalysis, this means that Lesbia's speech, by exposing impasses within the symbolic system we call language, marks the failure of that system. According to Lacan, gender comes into being when language fails, and it does so in two distinct ways: it either says too much, exposing the failure of language, or it says too little, hiding that failure. Of these, the latter is Lacan's masculine, the former his feminine. This basic premise is useful for reading the relationship between Catullus and Lesbia, and if we approach the Lesbia cycle within a Lacanian framework, we find that Catullus consistently presents Lesbia's speech on the outskirts of language. Lesbia's speech highlights those instances where language fails to convey meaning.

In "Sappho's Poem/Get a Job" Lesbia is said to be "laughing sweetly" (line 6). Laughter makes noise, and it has the potential to convey

---

[28] This is particularly odd because other Roman poets such as Ovid and Propertius do give voice to female characters. See, for example, Propertius 1.3.35.

[29] Jacques Lacan (1901–1981) is a French psychoanalyst and psychiatrist whose work has had a significant impact on literary theory and whose theory of gender is particularly helpful for understanding the presentation of gender in the Catullan corpus.

[30] For an excellent introduction to Lacan's presentation of sexuality, see Joan Copjec, *Read My Desire* (MIT Press, 1994) or Juliet Mitchell and Jacqueline Rose, eds., *Feminine Sexuality: Jacques Lacan and the école freudienne* (W. W. Norton and Company, 1985).

meaning, but it is not language per se. Likewise, in "Her Husband" (83) Lesbia "snarls and growls" (line 7). The Latin verb here is *obloquitur*, the root of which gives us "loquacious" in English, but Catullus uses the root with the prefix *ob-*, which means "to be in the way of." That is, etymologically speaking, Lesbia "gets in the way of language." Even when Catullus uses good Latin verbs of speaking, including *dicere* (to say), to characterize what Lesbia says, that speech ends up being unclear or suspect. "Once" (72) exploits a beautiful ambiguity in the rendering of reported speech in Latin that can make it impossible to differentiate between the subject and direct object of an indirect statement, necessitating our parenthetical line, "(or that Catullus alone knew you – which was it?)." In "Lying" (92), the speaker assumes that since he at once abuses and loves Lesbia, she must do the same – in essence, he reads her "no" as "yes." In "Legalese" (109), Lesbia has promised something to Catullus, and this promise seems to have had a vocal component, but the rest of the corpus forces us to interpret her promise as "I am lying."[31]

In contrast, Catullus presents his speaker as Lacan's masculine. Consider how the speaker responds to Lesbia's impossible questions, the questions of the feminine.

7 Kissings of You

You ask how many kisses, Lesbia,
would be enough:
as many as Cyrene's sands
where silphium sprouts
between the oracle of steamy Jove
and the sacred tomb of old Battus,
as many as the silent stars
that nightly guard the secret

---

[31] "I am Lying" is the subtitle of Micaela Janan's chapter on Catullus' epigrams in *When the Lamp is Shattered: Desire and Narrative in Catullus* (Southern Illinois University Press, 1994), and anyone familiar with Janan's work will recognize her influence on my interpretation and my debt to her.

> loves of men.
> For infatuate Catullus,
> that number is enough
> which voyeurs
> cannot count, tongues cannot bewitch.

No finite number of kisses would be enough for Catullus – he's infatuate and insatiable – in Latin, he's literally "insane" (*vesano*). Lesbia's question pushes Catullus to the point where language fails. In fact, this poem at its heart is about the impossibility of expressing the infinite in language. Nevertheless, Catullus' speaker gives answer after answer, asserting his ability to quantify the infinite and denying the failure of language: "as many as Cyrene's sands," "as many as the ... stars." Catullus' answers necessarily say too little, which is symptomatic of the speech of Lacan's masculine, where Catullus' speaker lives. Lesbia's speech shows that she is ultimately unavailable to Catullus; despite the fact that Catullus can "be a man" in language (if not in life), he will never be able to know or possess Lesbia completely.

In the Lesbia cycle, Catullus presents his poetic concerns and defines his voice. If we look beyond its presentation of an erotic relationship between specific people, real or imagined, we shall appreciate the significance of the Lesbia cycle for Catullus' poetic project as a whole. The reason Lesbia is so compelling for us in the modern world is that her name refers not to a single woman but to those many fleeting things human beings pursue: love, art, identity. The Lesbia cycle, and indeed the corpus as a whole, is concerned with these basic desires of human experience. With the Lesbia cycle, Catullus not only crafts for the reader a thematic thread for his diverse corpus, but in the cycle he sums up the many elusive things human beings want with one word – Lesbia – a reference to the singular, fragmentary, sublime, nearly immortal and yet always unknowable original Greek poet herself: Sappho.

Lesbia may even stand for immortality. The polytheistic Greeks and pre-Christian Romans had nothing like a modern Western notion of afterlife. The earliest Greeks imagined that life after death was a wraith-like existence of eternal suffering. In Homer's *Odyssey*, for instance, Achilles tells Odysseus that he would rather be a servant indentured to a dirt farmer on earth than lord of all the dead in Hades (11.487–491).[32] During the Hellenistic period a number of so-called mystery religions promised initiates a different sort of life after death, but the specific beliefs of these religions are far from clear. Nor can we profitably compare the concept of the Elysian Fields (Isles of the Blessed) to normative Christian notions of heaven because, according to Vergil, the Elysian Fields were peopled only by the most elite of heroes. Ancient poets from Sappho to Martial, however, conceived of *poesis*, poetry-making, as a vatic pursuit and of their poetry as something that could lend them a form of immortality. As Sappho wrote, "Although they are only breath, the words that I command are immortal" (Barnard poem 9).[33] In the final line of Ode 1.1 Horace claims that his poems "will lift his lofty head to the stars" (*sublimi feriam sidera vertice*), and in the opening line of Ode 3.30 Horace likewise says that with his poetry he has "built a monument more lasting than bronze" (*exegi monumentum aere perennius*). Martial muses, tongue-in-cheek, "If I must die to get my fame, I gladly will put off the same".[34] Catullus himself prays in the final lines of "Dedication," "so take this book, whatever sort it is,/ and, dear Muse, let it last."

---

[32] My reference here is to the Greek. See Homer. *Odyssey;* translated by Robert Fagles (Penguin Classics, 1999) (11.554ff) or Stanley Lombardo (Hackett Publishing Company, 2000) (11.510ff) for translation.

[33] Mary Barnard and Dudley Fitts, *Sappho: A New Translation* (University of California Press, 1958).

[34] Horace, my translation. Garry Wills, *Martial's Epigrams: A Selection* (Viking Adult, 2008), 5.10.

THE POEMS

I

DEDICATION

To whom do I give my witty little book,
newly buffed and pressed?
To you, Cornelius: your singular audacity
consigned to three sheets the history of the world –
pithy but damned belabored.
You always thought my little nothings something,
so take this book, whatever sort it is,
and, dear Muse, let it last.

2ab

ATALANTA

※

Bird, little toy of my love,
the one she teases and holds close,
provokes to nip and bite when the heat demands diversion,
distraction from desire to soothe the burning ache
(at least that's how I see it):
if only I could play with you like that,
relieve the pain of wanting her ...
    ... this would be my golden apple
like the one that freed a nimble maiden
from a chastity belt so long bound tight.   10

3

DIRGE

Venuses and Cupids, Lovers and Literati,
Mourn!
Dead is my love's little fetish,
the bird she cherished
more than life.
He was delicious
and knew her to the quick.
Never leaving her lap,
hopping about
he'd chirp only for her.   10
Now he commences the shadowy journey
whence no bird returns.
Shame on you, shady henchmen
of Orcus
feasting on beauty: from me
you have snatched a bird of great price.
Evil deed, wretched bird:
you streak red
the swollen little eyes of my love.

4

PERSONIFICATION

Friends, that pirogue claims
to be the fastest of all boats,
claims it could outpace all other ships
by oar or by sail. It says
the driving Adriatic will confirm this,
as will the Cyclades, grand Rhodes
and Marmara, stiff with Thracian storms,
along with the sullen Pontic gulf
where that skiff was once a comate
branch whose greeny whispers issued   10
forth from the Cytorian ridge.
Cities of the Black Sea,
this boat says it is known best by you,
claims to have stood on your heights,
dipped its little blades in your waters
and from there to have born its master
through countless impossible straits
whether winds blew starboard or port
or Jupiter struck both sheets.
When finally it left the sea for this quiet pool   20
it made no vows to the gods of *terra firma*.
That was long ago: now in tranquil old age
it offers itself to you, Castor and Pollux.

5

TIME AND NUMBER

Lesbia, let's live and love and not admit
the old folks' worthless gossip.
Suns rise and set, but
for us there's one brief day
then one perpetual night.
So kiss me a thousand times,
then a hundred;
kiss me again a thousand,
then a hundred; kiss till
we're confused and cannot know   10
and none can count the number of our love.

6

KISS AND TELL

Flavius, I don't know
what kind of diseased little skank
she is, but your girlfriend must be
a sorry sight – and dumb –
if you're too embarrassed to kiss
and tell. You might be silent,
but you're not celibate;
your bedroom screams it:
garlands and perfume from Syria,
cushions and pillows strewn about,   10
and the groans and grindings
of your bed, pounded till it can hardly stand.
Keeping quiet wins you nothing. Why?
You wouldn't look so used up
if you weren't up to something.
Whatever you've got, good or bad,
tell me: I need you and your exploits
for an exalted, elegant poem!

7

KISSINGS OF YOU

You ask how many kisses, Lesbia,
would be enough:
as many as Cyrene's sands
where silphium sprouts
between the oracle of steamy Jove
and the sacred tomb of old Battus,
as many as the silent stars
that nightly guard the secret
loves of men.
For infatuate Catullus,   10
that number is enough
which voyeurs
cannot count, tongues cannot bewitch.

8

IT'S OVER

Catullus, you're pathetic.
Stop embarrassing yourself:
open your eyes.
You had your Golden Age,
prancing like a schoolgirl after that whore,
like no man ever did nor will again.
When she was game, you played everything
she'd allow –
you had your Golden Age.
Now she's unwilling and you're unmanned.   10
Don't pant after rejection, crave humiliation;
be strong; keep your head.
Goodbye, love – *now* Catullus is strong.
He won't ask, won't beg.
But you, you'll be wretched
when no one cares.
What's left for you?
Who will want you? Who will think you're worth it?
Who will you kiss? Who bite?
But you Catullus, come on: be a man.   20

9

ADVENTUS

Veranius, best of all my friends
by degrees of thousands,
have you really come home to your gods,
your dear brothers and elderly mother?
You have, and what precious news
that is to me. Will I see you safe
and hear you tell the story of Spain:
its environs, history, and people
as only you can, and clasping your neck
kiss your sweet mouth and eyes?   10
Of all the happy men in the world,
who is happier or luckier than me?

10

THE WHORE

Varus took me from the Forum
to meet his girlfriend – I had the time –
I could tell she was a little whore
but with a certain sex appeal, charming,
almost. At her place, questions came up:
what Bithynia was like,
how things looked there,
whether I had made any money.
I told it like it was:
Bithynia's   10
a bust for locals and provincials,
even for soldiers:
how anyone
padded his wallet with that butt-fuck governor
was beyond me: he just didn't give a shit.
"But really," they said, "what about the local product: boys?
You must have bought boys for your litter!"
"Well," I replied, winking at the girl,
"Bithynia wasn't so bad that I couldn't buy eight strapping boys!"
Of course, there was no one anywhere   20
willing to lift even my old couch by its spindly legs.
And the slut, true to form, called my bluff:
"Oooooh! Catullus, *darling!* Lend them to me, please:
I simply *must* visit the Temple of Serapis!"
"Hold on," I told the girl, "I misspoke just now ...
my buddy Cinna, I mean ... Gaius ... he bought the boys.

What's it to me if they're his or mine?
I use them as my own, but you, you whore,
you're so clueless and annoying
I can't even play a little."   30

II

MESSAGE TO MY LOVE

Furius and Aurelius, friends of mine –
whether Catullus is on the outskirts
invading Indians on Aurora's echoing shore
or penetrating Persians or soft Arabs,
Scythians or Parthian sharp-shooters,
crossing seas tinged by the gaping Nile or the high Alps,
taking it all in Caesar's wake,
the Gallic Rhine or the terrible Brits on the final frontier,
ready to master anything,
following the will of the sky –   10
relay a little venom to my darling:
Let her live with her boy toys and enjoy
breaking their balls again and again,
loving none;
let her bid Catullus goodbye
since she has clipped our love
like a bloom on the field's edge
cut short by a passing plow.

12

NAPKIN THIEF

※

Backhanded Asinius, you misuse
your hand when you lift the napkins
of guests lost in wine and talk.
You think you're witty? Fool,
it escapes you how tiresome
you are, how banal.
You think I'm wrong? Then listen
to your brother: he'll gladly pay
to stop your thieving – that boy's
nothing but wit and charm.   10
So either expect endless invective
or return my napkin,
not because it was expensive
(it has sentimental value).
My friends sent it from Spain,
and I love it as I love them,
Fabullus and darling Veranius.

13

BYOB

※

You'll dine well at my place,
Fabullus, if you bring a nice
meal and some wine, your wit,
a pretty girl, and your best stories,
not to mention a little luck.
And if you do, my friend,
you'll dine well, for Catullus
has a purse full of cobwebs!
In exchange you'll get love –
pure, unmixed – and something   10
even sweeter and more elegant:
I have for you the scent
Venus gave my Lesbia,
and when you smell it,
you'll pray to be one giant nose.

14

THE GIFT

Calvus, darling, if I didn't love you
so dearly, I'd hate you like Vatinius does,
all because of this gift. What did I do
or say to make you finish me off
with poetry like that? May the gods
give a world of hurt to whatever
client sent you such an insult!
But if, as I suspect, that scholar Sulla gave
this unique and unprecedented gift to you,
then it's a happy thing and worth it!   10
Damn, what a horrible, earnest little book
to send your own dear Catullus, and on
Saturnalia, too, his favorite day of the year!
This isn't over, genius. At first light I'll run
to the library and collect all the schlock and
drivel I can find: Caesius, Aquinus, Suffenus,
and I'll pay you back with these. Meanwhile,
book, get the hell out! Be gone, back to
the poets who formed your misshapen feet,
appalling poets, age of trouble!   20

14b

INTRODUCTORY FRAGMENT

If you ever read my little ineptitudes,
if you won't bristle at coming near ...

15

THIS ONE BOY

Aurelius, I entrust myself and my love
to you. I ask a simple favor:
if you ever desired something pure and chaste,
keep this boy safe, not from the crowd –
I don't fear those milling about the market
occupied with their own affairs –
I fear you and your assaulting cock
on behalf of all young boys.
Have at them, whichever you want
as you wish, as much as you can   10
when you're on the prowl, but –
I need this one boy chaste, please.
And if your lust and bad intent
force you to seduce my love
with tricks, you lowlife, what misery awaits!
Once your feet are bound, mullet
and radishes will stretch your gaping ass.

16

PERSONA

I'll fuck you in the mouth and ass,
Furius and Aurelius, you pair of fags.
You think I'm like my lines,
a little too soft, too flamboyant?
Sure, a man should control himself
but not necessarily his verses
which have only wit and charm
if they are sexy and supple
and can get a rise
not just from boys but from hairy old men   10
whose dicks are dull and stuck.
You think I'm a pussy
when you read my "thousand kisses"?
I'll fuck you in the mouth and ass!

17

HOMETOWN HERO

Verona, my hometown, you want to party
on your long bridge, you're ready to dance, but
you fear those spindly legs, tired for years,
will finally fall supine into the swamp:
May you get the bridge of your dreams;
may you sing from it your songs;
just allow me a bit of sport when you do:
I'd like a fellow Veronese vaulted ass over
teakettle from that bridge into the swamp
where the stinking pool is blackest   10
and the chasm especially deep.
The guy's a living insult, the intellectual junior
of a toddler asleep in his father's arms.
When he married a mere babe,
a bride greener than jailbait,
she begged to be watched like a juicy grape;
he gave her freedom to play,
didn't care, didn't tend his babe; now
the old trunk lies felled in a ditch, cut
by Ligurian bronze, perceiving everything   20
as if nothing at all were happening!
That fool of ours sees nothing, hears nothing,
knows nothing, not even who he is, or *if* he is –
I want him thrown straight from the bridge
into the muck: perhaps that will shock the old
dullard; perhaps he'll lose his spineless self
in the marsh like a mule loses
its iron shoes in the quicksand.

THIS ONE BOY II

Aurelius, king of gluttons once and future,
you want to fuck my love, and you don't hide it.
You're always there, flirting;
you hang on him, try every line
but all in vain: I'll snag you
before you set the snare.
If you weren't so skilled I'd shut up,
but now the boy has learned lust
and thirst – lay off, and I'll lay off;
if not, you'll find me up your ass.   10

22

OUR BACKPACKS

That Suffenus, the one you know well,
Varus, may be charming, urbane, sharp,
but his verses go on and on: I think
he's written thousands, perhaps more,
and I'm not talking drafts but
new books of heavy paper,
bossed and wrapped,
tied in red, plumbed with lead and
polished flat. As you read them,
that witty pretty boy becomes   10
a goat-milker, a common ditch-digger
so far removed is he, so changed.
Why? Whoever seems droll (or more practiced
than droll) is duller than dull when he writes;
there's no one more earnest than when he writes verse:
he entertains himself, marvels at his own talent.
We all commit this folly; no one's not a Suffenus
sometimes. And it's easy to see why:
we're all blind to the packs on our own backs.

23

DRY AND CRISP

You've neither slaves nor savings,
Furius: no bugs, no spiders, no fire,
just a father and stepmom whose teeth
crush stone! You live swimmingly
with your dad and his wooden wife;
it's no surprise you're all thriving:
you digest well and fear nothing,
not fire, not ruin, not theft and murder,
not anything else.
Your bodies are drier than horn   10
(or something even drier) parched by
heat, cold, and hunger.
What could be better?
You've no sweat, no saliva,
no bodily fluids of any kind.
And what's even more elegant,
your asshole's crisper than salt –
you don't take ten shits a year,
each one a little stone, a dry bean:
if you rubbed them in your hand,   20
you wouldn't even soil your fingers.
Don't deny how lucky you are, Furius,
don't be ashamed, and stop begging
for a loan.
You're fortunate enough.

24

JUVENTIUS

You're the flower of your family,
Juventius: present, past, and future.
Better to give away the wealth
of Midas than let yourself be loved
by one who has nothing. "But
he's attractive?" you ask. "Isn't he?"
Indeed, he's a beautiful pauper.
Make fun all you like, ignore my advice,
but the man has neither slaves nor savings!

25

THREAT

Fag-boy Thallus, softer than bunny fur,
softer than *foie gras* or a tender earlobe,
softer than the long-neglected limp dick
of an old man – Thallus, like a storm
of gluttony when Sloth puts suckers
to sleep. Thallus, return the cloak
you pinched, my Spanish napkin,
and the foreign engravings you display
as your own heirlooms, you idiot!
Return them, pried from your sticky fingers,   10
or my smoking whip will lash invective all over
your soft little ass and your girlish hands
while you thrash like a skiff on the raging sea.

26

ENCUMBERED

Furius, your little villa is liable –
not to the south wind nor the west,
not to savage north or easterly gales –
but to a mortgage of fifteen and change:
what a brisk, pestilent wind!

SYMPOSIUM

Slave boy, mixer of wine,
bring me a stronger glass
of the old Falernian! It's the rule
of our hostess Postumia,
soaked like a grape herself. Water,
enemy of wine, run off wherever you will:
find a more tiresome party. This one's pure Bacchus!

28

IN SERVICE

Friends of Piso, you worthless bunch,
little knapsacks at the ready,
how's it going? Dear Veranius,
Fabullus, darling, have you had enough
of that loser, the cold, the hunger?
Are the losses as good for you
as they were for me under Memmius?
Ah, Memmius, you fucked me over me so well,
so slowly, and for so long, pinned down
as I was by every last inch of you.   10
I know how it works; your case is similar:
you're choked by a cock just as big.
Is this how you better yourselves?
May the gods curse you both,
affronts to the *mos maiorum*.

29

THE SPENDTHRIFT

Are you watching this, Romulus?
Who but a greedy, lecherous shyster
could endure Mamurra enjoying
the fruits of Gaul and Britain?
Romulus, fag-boy, do you see this?
And you allow it?
That overweening tool works through
bed after bed like some love cock,
some Adonis.
Romulus, fag-boy, are you watching?   10
And you allow it? You're a greedy,
lecherous shyster.
Was it for this, dear Caesar, that you
went all the way to Britain, so
that fucked-out little prick could eat
up the profits? What kind of
backhanded charity is this? Hasn't he
ploughed through enough?
He spent his father's money,
then the Black Sea booty, then   20
our Spanish gold: now we fear
for Gaul and Britain.
Must you foster this scourge?
What does he do but burn money?
Pompey and Caesar, most pious leaders,
do you risk all of Rome for his sake?

30

FORGETFUL

🙎

Forgetful Alfenus, false
to your very best friends,
can nothing inspire you now
to pity your sweet beloved?
Do you betray me now,
deceive me so readily, backstabber?
The lies of the faithless displease
the gods: you neglect them
and me in my time of need.
Tell me why men betray   10
those who trust: you
promised my soul protection,
led me to think you were safe.
Now you take it back, scatter your vows
on cirrus winds.
You forget, but the gods do not:
Faith herself remembers and will
make you regret your crimes.

31

NOSTOS

Sweet Sirmio, of all islands and
peninsulas anywhere on flat water
or Neptune's vast expanse,
none do I glimpse so happily,
so willingly. I scarcely
believe I see you, not one but
two Thynias left behind!
What's better than cares dissolved
when the mind puts down its bags,
weary from business abroad,   10
and regains hearth and home,
a familiar bed? Homecoming
is the reward of labor.
Greetings, lovely Sirmio,
Celebrate with your joyful master!
And you, Etruscan lake, laugh
at a homespun joke.

SWEET IPSITILLA

Please, Ipsitilla, my darling,
my charm, demand my presence
at noon. If you do (and if you please),
be sure the door's open, and
don't go out but stay home:
prepare for nine consecutive
fuckings. If you can,
call me now: I'm in bed
full, lying flat and
pitching a tent.   10

33

FAMILY BUSINESS

🐍

Vibennius and Femme, bathhouse
punks extraordinaire: the father's
filthy hand raised a son with a
greedy asshole. Get the hell out of Rome:
the father's crimes are known,
and the son's ass too hairy to sell.

34

DIANA'S SONG

We belong to Diana,
girls and chaste boys:
chaste boys and girls,
we sing Diana.

Diana Latonia, queenly
Daughter of Zeus,
birthed at the olive tree,
we sing Diana.

Mountain mistress at the
gates of sylvan green,   10
secret glen, sounding stream,
we sing Diana.

In childbirth, you are Juno Lucina,
other times bold Trivia or
the borrowed light of the moon:
we sing Diana.

Dividing the year by menses,
you fill with good fruit
the farmers' rustic lofts:
we sing Diana.   20

Whatever name you choose,
protect the children of Rome
as you did in days of old:
we sing Diana.

35

UNFINISHED

Poem, please tell Caecilius, love poet
of my heart, to exchange Lake Como
for Verona: I must discuss with him
the notes of a mutual friend.
If he's wise, he'll eat the road
though a thousand times his sweetheart
calls him back, begs him to delay,
her arms around his neck.
If I have the story straight, she's
been helplessly in love since reading   10
his unfinished "Cybele," whose
subtle flames singed her to the bone.
I understand: she's got better taste
than Sappho's Muse; if he finished it,
it would be charming.

36

INTO THE FIRE

Shitty scraps of Volusius,
secure my love's vow:
to Venus and Cupid she swore –
provided I apologize,
stop brandishing my polished insults –
that she would consecrate to the limping god
a burnt offering:
the best of the very worst poetry.
She, the worst girlfriend of all,
thought she'd charm the gods with her sham –   10
now, Aphrodite, Seafoam Goddess of Idalion
and Urion by-the-sea,
Ancon and stalky Knidos, Amathos and Golgi
and Dyrrachion, Ocean's pub,
reckon her debt as paid, if that's not base or coarse –
and you, shitty scraps, countrified crap
Volusius calls poetry, leap into the fire.

CATHOUSE TAVERN

Patrons of the Cathouse Tavern,
nine doors from Castor and Pollux,
you think you're the only cocks
fitted to fuck these girls?
You think the rest of us goats?
You – one or two hundred – sit there
contented fools. You think
I wouldn't fuck the lot of you?
Think again: I'll assault the brothel door
with graffiti. My girl, loved as no other,   10
for whom I struggled and fought,
fled from my bed to this place.
The nobles love her, pretty aristocrats,
and also – it's shameful – two bit, backstreet
adulterers: you, Egnatius, worst
of the hairy bunch,
son of bunny-soft Spain,
display in your dark beard
teeth whitened with urine.

38

CONSOLATION

※

Your Catullus is suffering, Cornificius,
suffering terribly, by god,
more and more each day, every hour.
Why don't you offer comfort?
It's the easiest thing in the world.
I'm upset, and this is how you show your love?
A little poem would help,
something especially weepy.

39

DR. TEETH

Egnatius always smiles to
show off his sparkling teeth.
In the courtroom when the
defense inspires tears, he grins.
If a mother burying her only son
mourns at the pyre, he smiles.
Whatever it is, wherever he is,
he shows his pearly whites.
This disease is neither elegant
nor urbane. I warn you, Egnatius,   10
if you were Roman or Sabine,
Tiburtine, Umbrian, Etruscan,
or a toothy Lanuvian,
even Transpadane, where I'm from,
if you were anyone at all
who brushed his teeth hygienically,
I'd still abhor your smile:
you laugh like a bitch.
But you're a Spaniard. In Spain,
each morning's piss is used to polish teeth   20
and rosy gums: the whiter your teeth,
the more piss you've drunk.

40

IMPALED

What misguided impulse, Ravidus
led a sorry specimen like you
to skewer yourself on my iambs?
Which god's misinterpreted omens
suggested this futile brawl?
What were you thinking?
Did you crave my vulgarity, or
were you after your fifteen minutes?
You'll find them in a long, punishing
poem, since you tried to fuck my lover.   10

41

FORMIANUS' GIRLFRIEND I

Ameana, that used-up whore,
that hawk-nosed slut,
wants a thousand bucks
now that her guy's gone bust.
If anyone cares, listen up:
that girl needs serious help;
She's half gone, and worse,
she's forgotten what she's worth.

42

LIGHT INFANTRY

Come here, my little verses,
all of you everywhere, as many as
there are: line up! This dirty slut thinks
I'm a joke, refuses to return my
books, if you can believe it. Let's
track her down, demand them back.
Who is she, you ask? That one:
strut like a cheap whore,
bark like a bitch from the sticks.
Surround her! Capture my poems!   10
"Give back my lines, you filthy cunt,
filthy cunt, give back my lines!"
You don't give a shit?
Diseased hole (or something worse):
We must do more than ask!
If nothing else, we'll make the bitch blush.
Shout now in a louder voice,
"Give back my lines, you filthy cunt,
filthy cunt, give back my lines!"
We've accomplished nothing.   20
Perhaps we should change our approach,
try something like this:
"Fair and proper maiden,
please return my lines."

43

FORMIANUS' GIRLFRIEND II

Hey, Bigfoot, Hey, Pinocchio!
You washed-out, dumpy, slobbering,
slow-witted hole of the homeless:
Do rednecks praise you, compare you with Lesbia?
Of course: these days, backwoods bastards reign.

44

AT TIVOLI

Our villa, whether Sabine or Tiburtine –
my friends know it's Tiburtine, but those
with a grudge insist it's only Sabine –
wherever it is, there I nursed a
terrible cough, reward from
my stomach for overindulging.
(Hoping for an invite, I read the
entire noxious speech Sestius wrote
against Antius: immediately
a chilling cold shook my lungs,   10
and I fled to your embrace,
your leisure and your nettles.)
Health restored, I give thanks;
you never blamed me. This time
it was my fault, but if I receive
another toxic text from Sestius,
let him get this plague: he didn't
invite me till I read his deadly prose.

45

ACME AND SEPTIMIUS

Septimus, holding Acme on his lap,
said, "My darling, if I don't love you
desperately, if I'm not prepared to
love you for all my years, may I
perish alone in Libya or become a morsel
for a grey-blue lion in thirsty India."
When he spoke, Love approved in every way.

Acme, luscious mouth tinged with grape,
turned to kiss the eyes of the boy drunk
on her: "You are my life, Septimius.   10
Let us serve this single master. A desire
finer and even more insistent burns in my soft marrow."
When she spoke, Love approved in every way.

Joined in mutual agreement, they
love and are loved. Septimius, aching,
prefers Acme to Damascus and London.
Septimius alone is Acme's pleasure
and delight. Are any lovers luckier,
any Venus more auspicious?

46

LEAVING BITHYNIA

Spring returns warm-thawed days;
the tumult of winter sky grows still
in the wake of tender Zephyr.
The Phrygian fields must empty,
Catullus, the rich fields of Nicaea
steam in summer: let's go to Turkey.
The impatient mind rushes,
eager feet fidget. Farewell, sweet
companions: different paths carry
home those who left as one so long ago.   10

47

PASSED OVER

Porcius and Socration, aka
"Scab" and "Famine,"
Piso's left-hand men, did
that trim-cut little prick
choose you over my boys
Veranius and Fabullus?
Are you lazing away at parties
all day while my boys wait
at the gates for their dinner?

48

INSATIABLE

If I could, Juventius, I would kiss your
sweet eyes three hundred thousand
times and never be satisfied,
not even if my kisses were
denser than grains in the granary.

49

CICERO

Cicero – most eloquent descendant
of Romulus, many as there are
or were or ever will be – Catullus,
the worst of all poets, gives great
thanks to you: by the same measure
as he is the worst, you are the best
of all lawyers.

EROTICA

Yesterday, Licinius, when we played –
we both felt it –
making sweet verse,
flirting with beats back and forth,
harmonizing, warm with wine.
Singed by your wit, I left
unfastened, overcome:
no relief in food or sleep,
I knotted the sheets,
longing for sunrise and you.   10
Spent and sprawled, limp,
I wrote this poem:
be kind, darling, and beware,
lest Nemesis exact her price;
she's a holy terror: don't piss her off.

SAPPHO'S POEM/GET A JOB

To me he seems a god –
that man, if man he is,
seems to surpass the gods,
who sitting close
sees you,
hears you laughing sweetly:
the moment I glimpse you, Lesbia,
sensation rends me and nothing remains …
                … my tongue sticks,
needling flames lick my bones,   10
my ears ring, eyes fade to double-black.

It's doing nothing, Catullus, that torments you:
in leisure your passions roam and writhe.
Leisure ruined kings of old and cities blessed.

52

CORRUPTION

What keeps you, Catullus? Why not die
already? Nonius infects the curule chair;
Vatinius has perjured the consulship.
Why the delay, Catullus? Why don't you die?

53

IN COURT

When Calvus in awe had catalogued
the charges against Vatinius,
I laughed at some guy in the crowd
who held up his hands and shouted out praise:
"What a goddamn eloquent little prick!"

54

TURN OFFS

Otho's cock is a puny nothing.
And I would think that the filthy
backwoods thighs of Hirrus
or Libo's plain and simple farts
(if not all these things) would
turn off you and Fufidius,
that old leftover ...
my innocent little iambs
will burn you again, my singular liege.

55

HIDEOUT

Please, if it's not a bother, show
me your secret lair. We sought you
in the Campus Minor, Circus
Maximus, every bookstore, the sacred
Temple of Jove. In Pompey's piazza
I questioned every girl, but no one
looked guilty. "What the fuck?"
I shouted, "Find me Camerius,
you whores!" One said, totally
deadpan, "Here he is, between my   10
blowzy boobs." It's a labor of
Heracles to put up with you, but
you won't disclose your whereabouts.
Tell us where you'll be: be brave,
tell us, trust the truth. Have blonde
babes taken you hostage? A tongue
in a closed mouth forfeits the fruits
of lust. Venus loves an open mouth.
Or, if you wish, keep secrets from others,
as long as I'm party to your exploits.   20

56

LAUGHABLE

It's ridiculous, Cato, hilarious,
a feast for your ears and your wit:
laugh if you love Catullus!
It's a joke much too absurd:
I just saw a boy
fucking his girl and split him
from behind with my shaft!

57

A PERFECT MATCH

They're a beautiful pair of perverts,
Mamurra the fairy queen and Caesar,
who likes it from behind. No wonder:
one stain matches the other perfectly,
one from the city, one from the coast,
they're here to stay. Equally
diseased, twins even, and
scholars between the sheets,
equally matched in greed and lust,
rivals both for and of the ladies: 10
They're a beautiful pair of perverts.

58

THAT LESBIA

Our Lesbia, Caelius, that Lesbia,
the one Catullus loved more than himself
and all others,
now in alleys and byways
shucks the noble cobs of Remus' progeny.

58b

CAMERIUS II

Even if I were Talos of Crete
or carried aloft like Pegasus,
or Ladas or swift-footed Perseus
or the white horses of Rhesus — add
to these all feather-footed flying fowl —
even if I sought the course of the winds,
which, Camerius, you might dedicate
to me, still I would be utterly bone tired,
devoured by exhaustion, my friend,
from searching for you!   10

59

LOW RENT

Bolognese Rufa, wife of Menenius,
sucks off Rufulus:
you'll find her in graveyards
stealing dinner from the pyre,
snatching bread, rolling free of flames,
catching a pounding
from the stubbly corpse-burner.

60

CLASSIC INSULT

Did a Libyan lioness or barking Scylla
spit you from the depths of a bitch-
dark womb so hard and foul that when
I ask for help in my final hour, you
hold me in contempt, iron-hearted?

WEDDING SONG (EPITHALAMION I)

Child of Helicon's Muse,
who steals tender virgins ripe
for a man: *God of Marriage,*
God of Marriage, sing the wedding song.

Gird your head with wreaths
of sweet and fragrant marjoram,
take up the yellow veil,
come hither on snow-white feet
glowing in shoes of gold.

Rise on that happy day singing,   10
voice ringing the wedding song.
Come with dancing feet;
shake the torch in your hand.

For Junia marries Manlius like
Venus come from Idalion
to meet Paris her judge:
fair maiden with omens fair,

fair as Lydian myrtle shining
on leafy branches, which
nymphs of the wood delight to   20
feed with dewy drops.

So come, Hymen, hurry!
Leave the Muse's caves
on craggy Helicon
cooled from above by the
icy streams of Aganippe.

Call the eager mistress to the
home of her new man, binding
her mind with love winding
here and there as ivy   30
enfolds a tree.

And you, virgin maidens,
for whom this day will come,
come and chant in time: *God of Marriage,*
God of Marriage, sing the wedding song!

Hearing that he is desired,
more gladly will he come,
the one who enacts Venus' will,
the one who joins true loves.

What god is more invoked   40
by lovers or beloveds? What
heavenly god more worshipped?
God of Marriage, God of Marriage,
sing the wedding song!

The trembling father calls you;
virgins loosen their skirts.
A husband strains with anxious
ears to hear you at long last.

You grant to the hands of
a rough youth the little bloom   50
fresh from her mother's lap.
God of Marriage, God of Marriage,
sing the wedding song!

Venus is nothing without you,
Hymen: honor follows pleasure

only when you approve.
Who would compete with you?

Without you no home has heirs,
no parent counts a son. There's
power when Hymen approves: 60
Who would compete with Hymen?

Lands that lack your rites
cannot protect their borders. There's
power when Hymen approves:
Who would compete with Hymen?

Throw the doors wide open!
The bride is coming near!
See how the torches shake
their shiny locks?
. . . .   70
. . . .

. . . .
. . . .
Her modesty slows her;
hearing more she weeps
that she must go.

Stop crying, sweet bride:
no woman more beautiful
ever witnessed daylight
rise from Ocean's lair.   80

You're a lily in the
budding garden of a rich man.
As you delay, the day flees.
Let the new bride appear!

Let the new bride appear
if the time is right: hear our
words. Torches shake their fiery
locks. Let the new bride appear!

Your husband, devoted
and faithful, innocent of   90
disgrace, disdains to sleep
apart from your soft breasts.

As a pliant vine engulfs nearby
trees, he will be wound in your
embrace. The day flees:
let the new bride appear!

Oh bed, which for all ...

. . . .

. . . .

. . . .   100
... shining feet of the bed ...

What joys will come to your
groom: volatile night and
afternoon delight! The day flees:
Let the new bride appear!

Lift up the torches, boys,
I see the bridal veil!
Come and sing in time: *God of Marriage,
wedding song, hail, hail, hail!*

Let the wedding farce tell   110
its bawdy tale, and let the boy
beloved, rejected by his master,
give the children treats.

Give the children treats, *puer*
delicatus, since now you're idle!
You've had enough play:
now serve the marriage god;
hand out the treats!

Till now you disdained the country
girls, boy beloved; today you'll   120
get a hot shave. Poor little
slave boy, hand out the treats.

Groom, you've made no headway
abstaining from boy love; today
you must abstain." *God of Marriage,*
wedding song, hail, hail, hail!

We know he was allowed before:
for a husband the rules are different.
God of Marriage, wedding song,
hail, hail, hail!   130

Bride, don't deny your husband
lest he look elsewhere.
God of Marriage, wedding song,
hail, hail, hail!

Come, let your new home, blessed
and prosperous, serve you!
God of Marriage, wedding song,
hail, hail, hail!

Until white senility, shaking
its tremulous head, nods   140
at everything. *God of Marriage,*
wedding song, hail, hail, hail!

Lift your golden sandals
auspiciously over the lintel
and under the polished door.
God of Marriage, wedding song,
hail, hail, hail!

See the groom within, reclined
on purple couch, wholly intent
on you. *God of Marriage,*   150
wedding song, hail, hail, hail!

His heart's flame burns
as deeply as yours and
more completely. *God of Marriage,*
wedding song, hail, hail, hail!

Let go the girl's lovely arms;
she must go to her
husband's bed. *God of Marriage,*
wedding song, hail, hail, hail!

Fair wives long held by old   160
men, give the girl over to
marriage. *God of Marriage,*
wedding song, hail, hail, hail!

Now, groom, you may come:
your bride adorns the bedroom
golden-white like a fresh blossom.

And groom, so help me gods, you
are no less lovely: Venus did not
neglect you. Day flees: don't delay.

You have not lingered long: 170
already you are here. May

Venus favor your yearning,
your display of sweet desire.

Whoever wishes to count the
many love games you'll play
must first total the African
sands or glittering stars.

Play as you wish, and soon
give us children; such an old
name must always have heirs   180
replanted from the root.

I want a little Torquatus in the
lap of his mother, stretching
plump hands toward his father
and sweetly laughing.

May he clearly resemble his father,
be easily known by all, and confirm
with his face his mother's fidelity.

From a good mother like this
praise will accrue to the family   190
just as the singular fame of
Penelope glorifies Telemachus.

Virgins, close the doors:
enough play.
Newlyweds, live well;
devote yourselves to pleasure
while you're young.

62

BRIDAL AGON (EPITHALAMION II)
✥

Boys' Invocation:
It's evening, young men, rise up: long-
awaited Vesper finally lights the sky.
Now is the time to rise, leave
feasting behind. Already the bride is
coming; already the hymn is sung:
God of Marriage, God of Marriage, oh come!

Girls' Invocation:
Maidens, see the young men? Rise up
in reply! Evening shows its fire: 10
certainly this is clear! See how swift they leap,
leap with all intent? Their song is a sight to see:
God of Marriage, God of Marriage, oh come!

Boys:
Victory won't come easy, boys:
look how the maidens practice,
their efforts not in vain. Every
part is memorized, and no wonder:
they work with one mind focused.
Minds and ears divided, our defeat   20
would be deserved: victory loves toil.
Focus our efforts now; now they begin
to sing; now we must respond:
God of Marriage, God of Marriage, oh come!

Girls:
Vesper, what star alights more cruelly
on the sky? You pry the virgin from

her mother's arms still clinging and
hand her all unwilling to a lustful youth.
What enemy is harsher to a city captured?   30
God of Marriage, God of Marriage, oh come!

Boys:
Vesper, what happier fire ignites the sky?
You sanction with your glow the marriage
pacts men made and parents promised,
consummated not until your heat has risen.
What divine gift is dearer than this lucky hour?
God of Marriage, God of Marriage, oh come!

Girls
Marriage has taken one of our own, girls …   40

Boys:
… when you arrive, Vesper, watchmen take
their posts; thieves hide but are caught
when you change your name to Dawn.
Virgins love to curse you, but it's a sham:
in time they get what they silently want.
God of Marriage, God of Marriage, oh come!

Girls:
Like a secret bloom in a hidden garden
unknown to the flock, touched by no plow,   50
which winds caress, sun strengthens, rain opens,
many boys and girls have longed for that one:
when it withers, cut by a sharp nail, no boy
or girl wants it. A virgin is prized by all:
but when her chaste bud is lost, body stained,
she delights neither boys nor girls.
God of Marriage, God of Marriage, oh come!

Boys:
When a vine grows lonely in a barren field
and never lifts itself, never bears soft fruit   60
but bends body low under its own weight,
root and highest shoot entwined,
this one no farmer, no oxen tend.
If fortune weds this same vine to an
elm, many farmers, many oxen tend it.
As long as a virgin remains intact, so
long will she grow unkempt. When
she is ripe for marriage, she is dearer
to a husband, less vexing to a father.

Don't argue with such a man, virgin;   70
don't oppose your father's choice: father
and mother must be obeyed. After all,
your body is not all yours: a third part
is your father's, a third your mother's, a third
your own. Don't fight the odds: they gave
their rights and dowry to that man.
God of Marriage, God of Marriage, oh come!

63

WILD SIDE

Swept over high seas in a swift ship,
Attis touched eager foot to Phrygian glade,
approached the deep-crowned reaches
of the goddess. Possessed by raving frenzy,
straying from reason, he cut away
with sharp flint the burden of manhood.
Coming to, she sensed the missing piece
that still stained the earth with fresh blood.
With lily hands she seized a drum,
your drum, Cybele, your rites, and   10
shook with supple fingers its taut hide,
raised with trembling voice this song:

"Here, come here to the woods, Gallae,
wandering flock of Dindymenae,
like exiles seeking foreign lands,
you braved cruel seas,
now follow my lead.
Hating Love's chains,
you shed your sex,
now please the goddess with quickening steps.   20
Here, come here, and don't delay:
follow me to Phrygia,
follow to the house,
follow to the glade of Cybele herself
where cymbal shouts
where tympani sing
where curved reeds play
where holy ululation rings

where Maenads shake their ivy heads
where sacred rites breed sharp cries,   30
where the cohort flutters wild and
we must dance the ritual."

As Attis, a woman beginning, sang to
her companions, the company shrilled vibrato-
tongued, drums moaned, cymbals chimed, and
the chorus sought green Ida, feet hurrying.
Through dappled woods she rushed,
breathing hard, ecstatic, drumbeat-led
like a fleeing calf unaccustomed to the
yoke, and the eager Gallae followed her   40
fleet feet. They reached the lair of Cybele
finally spent from their task and seized
upon sleep from fasting: Hypnos
collapsed their lids with easy languor,
frenzy of dance lost to stillness.

When the Sun's gold eyes lit the ether
bright, rough earth and sea, scattered
the shadows of night with fresh hoof-beats,
Sleep woke Attis then quickly fled:
graceful Pasithea held her in her lap.   50
From this quiet place, still and sane, Attis
took her deeds to heart. Mind clear, she
saw where she was, felt the lack; dizzy,
reeling, she ran back to the shallows,
took in the vast expanse of sea
and with brimming eyes addressed
her home in broken voice:

"Dear country of mine, creator, mother
I left like a runaway slave, I bent my

steps to Ida where I found snow, the   60
frosty homes of wild things, and once
possessed, their shadowy lair.
Where, dear country, do I think to find you?
My pupils long to drink you in while
sense for some short time is mine.
Have I exchanged my home for this strange land?
Have I abandoned friends, possessions, parents?
Where is the forum, the stadium, the racetrack?
Where is the gymnasium? Misery, misery,
over and over I must lament.   70
What gender, what form is denied me?
I am woman, youth, ephebe, boy;
I was the flower of the gymnasium, pride
of oiled athletes. My door was crowded,
threshold warm. When I rose at dawn, my
home was wreathed in blooming garlands.
Am I now a priestess, a servant of Cybele?
Shall I be a Maenad, slice of my former self,
an unmanned man? Shall I inhabit greeny Ida's
crags, lead my life under snowy peaks   80
with stag and vagrant boar? Now I
mourn what I did; now I regret."

The sound spilled from blushing lips, carrying
its missive to the ears of the goddess.
Loosing the yoke from her lions and goading
the foe of the flock, she thus exhorted: "Go now,
go, and be ferocious; make him froth
and foam; bring him back to the glade on the
cadence of fury, he who longs to escape my rule.
Mark your back with your cruel tail, flog yourself,   90
make the wood resound with your raging roar,

shake the mane red-hot on your mighty neck."
Dire Cybele spoke and let the lion slip free.
As instructed, he spurred himself to action,
charging, screaming, tearing through
underbrush with swift paws till he came to the
misty white beach. There he spied gentle Attis and
made his attack. Wild, out of her mind, she fled
back to the woods, forever to serve the goddess.

Goddess, Great Mother Cybele, Mistress,   100
please keep your fury far from my home:
stir up others; drive them mad.

64

EPYLLION

&

Long ago a fir tree culled,
native-born, from the top of Mount Pelion
took to Poseidon's realm and plied
the River Phasis to the edge of the world
carrying the flower of Greek youth,
sturdy trunks themselves,
greedy for fame,
who braved salty shallows in
that swift ketch and dared to
snatch the Golden Fleece from Colchis,   10
striking cerulean water with still-green oars.
The goddess herself, Mistress of Athens' high
citadel, marrying pliant pine to an upturned keel,
fashioned a chariot borne upon the breeze
that dipped its rustic prow first
in Amphitrite's course.
And when the vessel spread the churning sea
and foam spewed white at the oars' twisting,
out of the shimmering abyss rose
untamed faces: watery Nereids,   20
stunned at the sight.
On that day mortals caught a glimpse
of divine grace as sea-nymphs
bobbed on the eddying deep,
breasts full and soft.
On that day Peleus burned for Thetis,
who consented to mortal marriage, and
Zeus himself saw the necessity of the

union. Heroes of old, god-like children
sprung from mortal beauty,   30
I shall always honor you in song:
but you, Peleus, pride of Thessaly,
were so honored that Father Zeus
relinquished Thetis, his own dear love.
Did that magnificent creature cling to you?
Did Tethys and Ocean, who holds
the whole earth close in briny embrace,
yield to you that deathless hand?
When the sun dawned on the wedding day,
the palace was overcome: all Thessaly   40
thronged the royal house, beaming,
joyful, bearing gifts.
Cieros was deserted; locals exchanged
Tempe, Crannon, and the walls of
Larissa for Pharsalian rooftops:
no one tilled the fields, oxen grew soft
at the neck, low vines lay neglected
by the curved mattock, bulls
left clods unturned, the
sickle failed to sculpt its leafy charge,   50
and rust scabbed over fallow ploughshares.
But the house of Peleus, wherever
its rooms led, was radiant with gold and silver.
Ivory lit the floor, cups the table,
and the palace rejoiced in the
glow of royal treasure.
In the center of the crowded hall
stood a bridal couch inlaid with
Indian ivory and draped with a coverlet,
purple with the stain of wine-dark murex   60

that chronicled in woven verse the
deeds of heroes long dead:

Ariadne, burned to the core
by raw desire, looks out from the
pounding shore of Naxos
and sees Theseus sailing away with his fleet,
not quite believing what she sees,
still groggy with treacherous sleep,
deserted on the lonely strand.
But young Theseus, forgetful,   70
tears through the shallows by oar,
fleeing, leaving empty
vows to the reckless gale.
The Minoan princess watches Theseus
like a stone Maenad on the wracked beach
as great waves of sorrow wash her away.
She does not braid her shimmering hair
or hide her thinly-veiled form.
Nor does she bind her creamy breasts,
but belt and ribbon and robes slip   80
down from her body
to the playful waves at her feet.
She cares for nothing but you, Theseus:
mind, body, soul, all are lost.
For as soon as Theseus, fierce hero,
left the ragged coast of Piraeus
and reached that island palace
with its harsh-judging king,
Aphrodite sowed her needling seeds
into the poor girl, left Ariadne weak   90
with unrelenting passion.
Athens, according to tradition,

laid low by a cruel plague,
gave as blood price for Androgeos
a yearly feast to the Minotaur:
the choicest boys and blossoming maidens.
Since such evil vexed his fledgling city,
Theseus wished to offer his own body
for that of his Athenians to
prevent corpse upon corpse   100
being carried away to Crete.
Blessed with a nimble breeze for his
light ship, he came to high-minded Minos
and his overweening halls.
One glimpse and the eyes of the princess caught fire,
though she slept chaste still, sweetly
breathing in the embrace of her mother
like new myrtle on the banks of the Eurotas,
like hues borne on the spring breeze,
but she indulged her ardent gaze until   110
flames utterly consumed her and
her very marrow ached.
You, Eros, who contaminate joy with sorrow,
light passion in a suffering breast,
and you, Aphrodite, Queen
of Golgi and verdant Idalion,
on what seas did you toss the mind of that stormy
girl panting after some blond stranger?
What fears harbored in a heart so beset?
How pallid did she turn, paler   120
than gold, when Theseus eager
to best the savage Minotaur
challenged Death for immortal fame?
Generous, she offered gifts and secret
vows to great avail:

Theseus took down the beast,
horns thrashing in vain, and
mastered his girth as a brute gale,
wrenching the wood with its blast,
masters the Taurian oak, branches protesting, or   130
fells the pine, its bark dripping with sweat,
torn from its very root,
exposed and broken to the core.
Then the hero turned on his heel,
basking in praise and holding fast
to the maiden's thread lest the blind confusion
of the maze hold him in its twisted depths.

But why do I, far diverted from my first tale,
recall how that maiden, leaving behind
the sight of her father, the embrace of   140
her sister and mother, who bereft
used to rejoice in the ill-fated girl, who
chose above all the sweet love of Theseus?
Or how she came to the foamy shores of Naxos
in the ship of her faithless husband
only to be left behind when her eyes succumbed
to sleep? They say that angry, heart ablaze, she
let forth cries, deep and clear, from her
breast, climbed steep mountains whence she
viewed the vast flux of the sea,   150
that she ran into salt waves lifting the
thin robe from her calves and, raining
cold sobs on wet cheeks, in
misery made the ultimate complaint:

"Is this how you leave me, Theseus, on a deserted
shore far from my home, you treacherous
bastard? Your leaving is forgetful, mindless

of the gods! Will you carry your
perjuries homeward? Can nothing bend
your cruel intent? Do you have no mercy, 160
no path to pity from that sour heart?
These are not the tempting things you promised;
you ordered me to hope not for this but
for wedding songs, a happy marriage:
useless hopes the violent winds dismember.
No woman should believe a husband's vows or
hope a man might speak the truth.
When a man wants something, he
fears nothing, promises anything. When
he's satisfied, he forgets his word, won't 170
hesitate to perjure. When you were caught
in death's whirlpool, spinning, I
snatched you out. I lost my brother rather
than desert you in your time of need.
In exchange my carcass will be carrion for
dogs and birds; in death I'll have no burial.
What lion bore you in a lonely cave? What sea
spat you from its fuming waves? To what Syrtes,
what gluttonous Scylla, what gaping
Charybdis do you owe your existence? If our 180
marriage was not to your liking, if you
bristled remembering the fierce advice of your
father, you could have led me home a
slave to serve you joyfully, pouring sweet
water over your feet, spreading your
bed with purple robes. Why do I complain
in misery to deaf winds, graced with
no sense, unable to hear or answer my voice?
Theseus is already halfway home, no mortal
with me on this empty strand. Vaunting too much 190

in our final hour, fortune cruel denies us one kind ear.
Omnipotent Zeus, I wish no Athenian ship
had touched the shores of Crete, no false
sailor ever brought dire tribute to
our unyoked bull, evil, masking brutal plans with
a beautiful face, a guest in our home!
What shall I do? Where is hope for the lost?
Should I seek the mountains of Ida?
An abyss of truculent sea isolates me.
Should I hope in my father, whom I left   200
to follow a man spattered by my brother's slaughter?
Shall I console myself with the true
love of a husband who's bending the heavy
oars in eager flight? Stranded without a house
on a wave-girded island, no exit lies open,
no escape, no hope: all is silent, all deserted,
death everywhere.
Nevertheless, let my lids not yet droop, let
sense not leave my tired frame till I beg
justice from the gods, pray for   210
heavenly help in my final hour.
Here, come here, Furies, vengeful
punishers, heads ringed with snaky
locks carrying anger on hissing tongues:
hear the cry curdled in my marrow,
impotent, burning, blind with rage.
These truths spring from my inmost breast:
don't let me suffer in vain.
Just as he left me alone, goddesses,
let him ruin himself and his family."   220

She poured this prayer from her distraught
soul, demanding retribution for

savage deeds, and the celestial judge
nodded his assent. The land and
white-capped waters shook; the
firmament rattled its glittering stars.
And Theseus let slip from the blind fog
of his mind and blank heart everything
once sown there, mandates once
held firm, and forgetting to hoist the   230
propitious sail, denied his sad father the
sight of a son's safe arrival at port.
Once upon at time, when Aegeus trusted to
the winds his son departing Athena's
gates, holding him close, he gave these
mandates: "Dear son, more precious to me
than long life, whom I must commit to
dangerous straits, son only just recovered at
the far edge of old age, my fate and
your fierce virtue rip you from   240
an unwilling father whose tired eyes
are not yet sated with the dear visage
of his son. I send you away rejoicing
not in my heart, nor will I allow
you to carry signs of good fortune. First,
fouling my head with dust, I will voice
my soul's lament and suspend from
your wandering mast dusky sails to herald
with Spanish dye our grief, our destruction.
If the goddess of Iton who guards Athens   250
and the descendants of Erectheus
allows you to dip your hand in taurine
blood, burn this in your heart's memory:
remember my mandates;
though time passes, don't forget.

As soon as you see our hills, let the
dark sails fall, and fly white from
woven ropes." These mandates he'd once
held firm abandoned Theseus like clouds
driven from a snowy peak by a gust of wind.   260
When his father sought a vantage point, anxious
eyes cloudy with tears, and saw the dark
sails he jumped headlong from the cliff
believing Theseus lost, and our hero
returned home to a father's funeral.
The grief he had brought to Ariadne
he now felt himself.

The maiden, watching him go, churned
her cares in a heart beset, but in another scene
lovely Bacchus hovered with a band of   270
satyrs and Sileni, struck by desire and looking
for you, Ariadne. His bacchants raged about,
minds possessed and heads tossing:
Euhoe! Euhoe!
Some shook spears tipped with pinecones;
some scattered the limbs of a calf;
some wound themselves with writhing
snakes; some performed mysteries
known only to initiates.
Others beat drums with open palms or   280
shrilled cymbals of tinny bronze; horns
blasted raucous sounds; a strange flute
screamed a bristling tune.

With such scenes was the coverlet
wrapping the bridal couch woven.
When the youth of Thessaly had taken
in their fill, they gave way to gods.

As rough Zephyr with a breath stirs
the calm face of the morning sea when
Aurora crosses the sun's lintel, moving   290
slowly at first with a mellow gust, laughter
singing gently, and gradually becoming stronger,
cresting catches the purple sunrise from afar:
thus leaving the royal court each one
took his leave by his own winding way.
After their exit came Chiron from the
heights of Pelion with woodsy gifts
the fields bear, gifts Thessaly grows
on high peaks, flowers the westerly breeze
births at water's edge: these he wove into   300
plaited garlands to delight the house with
a joyful bouquet. From Tempe, girded green
with pendant limbs, land celebrated in dance,
came Penios. He brought tall beech trees pulled
at the root, straight-backed laurels, swaying
plane trees, pliant poplar, sister of burnt-up Phaeton,
breezy cypress. He wove these in a broad
swath around the palace, creating a
living court roofed in soft leaves.
Trickster Prometheus followed bearing scars   310
of a punishment earned bound and hanging
from that rockface. Then came Zeus and
Hera with their divine children, leaving behind
only Phoebus in the sky and his mountain-
dwelling twin, both spurning Peleus and
refusing to celebrate Thetis' wedding.
They bent their limbs to bright seats at
tables laden with the feast while the
Fates, bodies shaking with age, presaged in song.
Their frail bodies were shrouded in white   320

tipped wine-dark at the hem; rosy crowns
graced snowy heads; hands spun endlessly
their ritual task, the left holding the distaff
wound with soft wool, the right
carefully forming the thread with fingers
supine then twisting on sloping thumb
the smooth-weighted spindle, snipping teeth
keeping the thread always even,
dry lips peppered with bits that lately
marred the fine thread: at their feet wicker   330
baskets kept soft fleeces of shining wool.
Combing these, they poured out divine
prophecy in clear-voiced song which
no later age will claim false:

"Hope of Emathia, dearest to Jove,
you who marry exceptional honor with
tremendous virtue, hear on this blessed day
what the sisters foresee for you.
You pulling the thread of fate,
Run, spindle, spindle, run, run!   340
Hesperus will soon deliver welcome
bridal gifts: with that lucky star your wife
will come, steeping you in love to bend
the soul, joining with you in languid
sleep, supple arms about your strong neck.
Run, spindle, spindle, run, run!
No home ever sheltered such love,
lovers never joined in such a pact;
as Thetis consents, so, too, does Peleus.
Run, spindle, spindle, run, run!   350
Born to you will be Achilles, fearless
son known to enemies by his firm chest

unyielding, a repeat victor on the long track
passing even the flame-footed stag.
Run, spindle, spindle, run, run!
No hero will surpass him when Phrygian
plains drip Teucrian blood and the
heirs of wily Pelops, besieging the city,
sack Troy's walls in a long, distant war.
Run, spindle, spindle, run, run! 360
Of his godlike worth and famous deeds mothers
will speak at the funerals of sons when
they let fall a lock from white head,
bruise sunken breasts with tired fists.
Run, spindle, spindle, run, run!
As a reaper thinning dense crops cuts
through a yellow field, heat blazing,
he will mow the sons of Troy with hostile scythe.
Run, spindle, spindle, run, run!
Witness to his worth will be Scamander, 370
racing to the Hellespont, whose course
will narrow in the warm crush of bodies,
deep waters clogged with gore.
Run, spindle, spindle, run, run!
Riches of war paid out will witness his
death when his barrow, heaped up
round, receives the white limbs
of a virgin struck down.
Run, spindle, spindle, run, run!
When fortune allows the tired Greeks 380
to break Neptune's wall at Troy,
the tomb will run with the blood of Polyxena
succumbing to the sword, knees buckling,
falling headless to the tomb.
Run, spindle, spindle, run, run!

Come, join in joyous love!
In pact auspicious let the husband
receive his goddess; let the bride
belong to her lover at long last.
Run, spindle, spindle, run, run!   390
At dawn her nurse will adorn her not
with yesterday's garland; her mother,
relieved that her daughter no longer
sleeps alone, will hope for dear grandsons.
Run, spindle, spindle, run, run!"

Forseeing such joys for Peleus, thus
sang the Fates from holy breasts
long ago when piety still lingered,
and divine beings visited the homes of worthy
heroes, showed themselves among mortals.   400
Zeus visited his splendid temple on
feast days, saw the hecatomb spread
yearly across the earth. Wandering
Bacchus led revelers from the top of
Parnassus, hair unbound when worshippers
rushed happily from every corner of Delphi
to the smoldering altars. On the battlefield
Grim-Reaping Mars, Mistress Athena
and Nemesis would exhort the troops.
But after the earth was drunk on crime and   410
mortals let go the desire for justice,
brothers poured fraternal blood,
the son stopped mourning his parents,
the father rejoiced at his son's death, eager
to have his lovely daughter-in-law,
and the godless mother seduced her innocent
son, ignoring affront to the household gods.

All things speakable, all unspeakable
were mixed with such wicked fury that
justice-minded gods departed: no longer do   420
they visit human assemblies or suffer
to be touched by mortal light.

65

LIKE AN APPLE

Pain, Hortalus, keeps me from my learned
mistresses, consumed by constant grief.
Nor can my mind deliver the sweet gifts
of the Muse, inundated as it is with misery:
Lethe's lapping waves have just washed
over the pallid feet of my brother,
pinned down by Troy and
hidden by Rhoetean sands …

… will I never see you again, brother
I loved so well? I will always adore you,   10
always write poems darkened by grief,
songs like Procne sang under thick branches
mourning the fate of Itys – nevertheless,
Hortalus, amid such sorrow I send
the translation below (lest you think your
words were trusted in vain to drifting winds or
slipped by chance from my mind) like an apple,
furtive missive of love, that bounces from
the chaste lap of the virgin who forgot it
in her skirts, and it rolls forth in a determined course   20
when she starts at the arrival of her mother,
a knowing blush staining her face with dismay.

66

CALLIMACHUS' LOCK OF BERENICE

Like one who has scanned the grand eyes
of the world, known the rising and falling
of stars, how the yellow blaze of the sun fades,
how stars set at certain times, known how
sweet love calls the Moon from her arc,
driving her to Endymion's cliffs, thus
Conon saw me on my starry threshold,
locks of hair from the head of Berenice,
shining richly, the tresses she promised god
after god, stretching tender arms to heaven   10
when her new royal husband left for
Syria still bearing sweet scars from
nocturnal battles he'd waged for virgin
spoils. Is Venus so hateful to brides?
Are tears that frustrate parental joys
and flood the bedchamber feigned?
I swear, gods, they mourn falsely: my queen
taught me this, moaning and mourning
her husband gone to grim battle.
Or was it the doleful loss of your   20
brother, not just your bed bereft?
How close to the bone grief cut:
the heart in your anxious breast
lost every sense! I saw in girlhood
you were strong, generous. Have you
forgotten the good deed that won you
the king, such deed as no one else dared?
How sad the farewell speech you gave,

all the while wiping away tears. What god
changed you? Or can't a lover bear to   30
be away from her lover's body?
You promised me to the gods, along
with a sacrificial bull, if they would return
safe your sweet love. Swiftly he added
captive Asia to the borders of Egypt.
And I, in light of these deeds and before
this heavenly assembly, discharge
old vows with gifts new. I left
your head unwillingly, my queen,
unwillingly, I swear on your crown. Let   40
she who vows vainly be punished, but
who can compete with shears? Even the
tallest mountain whose girth bright Helios
surmounts was conquered when Persians
unveiled a new sea and a young stranger's fleet
severed Mount Athos. What recourse has a lock
when mountains yield to the sword?
Zeus, curse the first miners to seek
veins in the earth and draw tight the strength
of iron. While my sisterly curls, recently   50
bereft, lamented my fate, Zephyr, windy
brother of Memnon, flying horse of Arsinoë
appeared, beating the air with nodding
wings, lifting me high into the nocturnal ether
and the chaste lap of Venus: Greek settler
on Canopic shores, she herself
called the horse to my rescue.
Lest on the prismatic threshold of
night only Ariadne's gold crown have the
place of honor, Venus also fixed me to shine   60
as I made my damp way to heaven,

devoted spoils of a flaxen head, young
star among the old. I turn in my course
near Virgo and Leo, joined with Lycaon's
Callisto and before late Boötes, who barely
falls to the sea. By night the tiptoes of
gods pass by. By day, the light of clear Tethys
is mine. If I may speak, Nemesis, so as not to
conceal the truth out of fear – even if the stars
eviscerate me with hateful words – I'll reveal   70
the sincere depths of my heart. I do not rejoice
at this turn of events that took me forever
from the head of my mistress. With her
(though deprived while she was a virgin)
I drank in a thousand scents. Torch-lit
brides, don't reveal your bodies
to your grooms, don't hand over bare-
skinned breasts from robes unbound till the
onyx box has poured its scented gift,
you who tend your vows in faithful beds.   80
(Whoever gives herself to adultery, let the
dust drink her gifts in vain and squalor: I
seek no gifts from those unworthy. Instead,
brides, may endless harmony and love
enduring keep your homes.) My queen,
when gazing at the stars on holy days you
supplicate Venus, deprive me not of
scent but rather treat me with gifts so
great the stars lament, "Let Orion shine
beside Aquarius: I'd rather be a royal lock!"   90

67

DIALOGUE AT VERONA

INTERLOCUTOR:
Greetings, Door, delight of the sweet
husband, delight of the father:
may Zeus favor you and those within,
door that served old man Balbus kindly
when he owned the house, door
they say cruelly served his son when
he was married and the old man dead.
Come, tell us why you changed,
why you turned against him.   10

DOOR:
It's not my fault (if it please Caecilius,
my new master) though it's said to be.
No one can find fault with me: it's true
what people say, "blame the door for
everything!" Whenever dirty dealings
are discovered, everyone shouts,
"Door, it's your fault!"

INTERLOCUTOR:
Your word's not enough: say it like you mean it!   20

DOOR:
How can I? No one cares about the truth.

INTERLOCUTOR:
I do, so don't hold your tongue.

DOOR:
First, whoever says she came here
a virgin lies. Her first husband
didn't touch her, that's true; his tender
member hung down softer than peach fuzz:
he couldn't get it up past his tunic, but   30
his father apparently slipped into bed
and stained his son's sad sheets
because his filthy mind was aflame
with lust or, since his son wasn't up to
the task, someone more upright had to
loosen her chastity belt.

INTERLOCUTOR:
What shocking piety in so extraordinary a father
to piss in the lap of his own son!

DOOR: 40
Brixia, town where the Mella flows
golden in gentle channels
at the foot of Cycnus' watchtower,
Brixia, mother of my own Verona,
confirmed it — and that she had affairs
with Postumius and Cornelius.
Someone will protest, "What?
How can you, a door, consummate
homebody, unable to eavesdrop,
fixed to the lintel, opening and closing   50
the house, know such things?"
I often heard her speak in furtive voice.
She confessed to her maids her crimes,
calling by name those I mentioned,
never supposing I had ear or tongue.
She added another man, too,

one I'd rather not name lest he raise
his red eyebrows. He's tall, and someone
once brought suit against him
on the trumped-up charge   60
he'd knocked her up.

68

ODE TO A FRIEND

Hard pressed by fortune and
cruel fate, shipwrecked, caught
in frothing waters, you sent me
a little epistle penned with tears,
hoping I might dislodge you
from death's door. Blessed Venus
gifted you no peace, no sleep
for your single bed, nor could the Muses
distract you with sweet songs of old:
your mind watched, anxious.   10
It's pleasing that you call me friend,
seek from me the gifts of verse
and love. Lest you be unaware
of my troubles and think I am put off
by your request, hear on what breakers
I am tossed, and seek your blessed
gifts from one less fraught.

From the time I donned my
toga, when life was spring at its best,
I had plenty of fun. The goddess   20
knows me, goddess whose cares are
all sweet bitterness. Death —
my brother's death — stole my zest.
My brother, snatched away, shattered
my content: our whole family is a tomb;
gone with him are the joys once nourished
by his affection. With him I lost

my mind, fled from avocation and delight.
Thus, when you write, "It's a bore that
you're in Verona, Catullus, since   30
anyone who's anyone there sleeps alone,"
it's no bore: it's misery. Forgive me
if I cannot deliver the gifts grief stole
from me: I am at a loss. And
there's no library here; I live
in Rome: there is only my home, my city,
the passing of my life. Of many
books I brought here just a few, so please
don't think my manner unkind or heart
untrue when I don't have either thing   40
you seek: you'd have them already if I did.

I can't keep silent, Muses, about how
this man helped me, how many ways he helped.
Lest time flying in this forgetful age cover
his zeal with blind night, I'll tell you,
Muses, and you tell countless future ages:
make this old papyrus speak!
. . . .
In death let his fame grow; let the
lofty spider weaving a fine web not   50
obscure his name with her work.
You know the cares Venus brought,
how duplicitously she teased when
I burned hot as Aetna's crags, hot as
hot springs at the Hot Gates, eyes
wasted from endless weeping, cheeks
pouring rain like a mountain stream
springs forth shining from mossy stone
(which, washed headlong from a sheer valley

makes its way through a city, sweet
solace to the voyage-weary traveler
when summer's weight cracks hard-
baked fields). Or like a following breeze
calms sailors tossed in a black storm when
they've prayed to Castor and Pollux:
such was his help to me. He opened freely
land once closed, gave to me and my
mistress a shelter for mutual love.

Here my splendid goddess turned her soft step
and stood, foot gleaming, bright sandal on
worn threshold the way Laodamia
once came burning with love to the house of
Protesilaus, a house established in vain
since sacred blood had not yet pacified the
heavenly host. Nemesis, let nothing be
pleasing enough to undertake rashly with
the gods unwilling. Her husband gone
before two winters' long nights had sated
their passion, Laodamia, forced to unclasp
the neck of her new husband, learned how
hungry is the altar for ritual gore, learned
that she was able to live bereft,
which the Fates knew she would be
if he set out for the walls of Troy.
After the loss of Helen, Troy summoned
the Greek kings. Unspeakable Troy,
communal grave of Europe and Asia,
bitter ashes of men and manly virtue, did
you even bring death to my brother?
Dear brother, snatched from me, bereft
himself of life's cheer, our whole family

is a tomb; gone with him are the joys
once nourished by his affection. He lies
far away with neither family graves nor
familiar ashes; foul Troy and soil alien
detain him, a hapless burial at world's end.
Rushing to Troy, the flower of Greek
youth is said to have deserted home and
hearth lest Paris enjoy unfettered time with
his adulterous prize in sheltered bed.   100
From you, lovely Laodamia, a marriage
sweeter than life or soul was taken.
At the pinnacle of love a sucking tide
drew you down into an abyss like the one
the Greeks say dried the rich ground
near Arcadian Cyllene when the swamp
was drained, the swamp Heracles
emptied, severing mountain marrow when he
pierced Stymphalian birds with precise
arrows at the order of a master far below   110
him till the door of heaven thrummed with
gods and Hebe lost her virginity.
Laodamia, your deep love was deeper than that abyss:
it taught you still untamed to bear the yoke.
Not even so precious to a parent racked by
age is the lone daughter who bears late
a dear grandson who, though scarcely
a youth, has his name inscribed atop the will,
heir to his grandfather's riches, steals
hope from that laughing-stock cousin,   120
and keeps vultures from the white head. Nor
to your love does the bliss of the dove compare
(whose eager beak is known to snatch

kisses more shamelessly than a whore).
You out-passioned them all, Laodamia,
once united with your blond mate.

My own darling, glowing in my lap
with the glint of Cupid's saffron robe
fluttering about her, held her own and more:
and if she is not content with Catullus alone,   130
let us bear her rare breaches of modesty and
be neither unsophisticated nor narrow-minded.
Remember that Hera, top goddess, checked
her seething anger at the indiscretions of Zeus,
knowing the many secrets of her lustful
mate. But it's not fair to compare men with
gods; and let go of familial duty, too: she came
to my house without imported perfumes,
led by no father's hand, and gave by night's
delight furtive gifts filched from her husband's   140
bed. It's enough that the day given only to me
she marks with a whiter stone.

Therefore, my friend, in exchange for your help
I gave what I could: a poem, lest today, tomorrow,
or the endless succession of days mar your name
with scabbing rust. The gods will add more gifts
like those Themis gave to the righteous in ancient times.
May you and your life, the house where we play,
and your love be lucky, you who first gave us
shelter, from which all good things come, and   150
far above that, this gift which is dearer to me than
myself: my darling, with whom living life is sweet.

69

NO BEAUTIES FOR THE BEAST

Rufus, don't be surprised that no girl
spreads her velvet thighs, not even
when you soften her with bribes of
jewels and gowns. An ugly tale
persists that goats inhabit your armpits.
Women fear this, and no wonder:
no beauty would sleep with such a beast!
Either slay that stink, or
stop asking where the ladies are!

70

WIND AND WATER

Lesbia wants to marry no one
more than me, not even if Jove
himself sought her. So she says,
but what a woman says
to an eager lover
should be written
on the wind and in running water.

71

MALODOROUS

If anyone deserves the stench of goat-pits,
if gimping gout wounds anyone deservedly,
it's that rival of yours, the one who takes
your love for a spin. He's a miracle of two
maladies; whenever he fucks, two are fucked:
she by the smell, he by the disease.

72

ONCE

You said, Lesbia, that you knew
Catullus alone
(or that Catullus alone
knew you – which was it?),
that you wouldn't trade me
for Jove himself.
I loved you then
not as the crowd loves an idol
but as a father loves his sons.
I know you now, and though I want   10
you more than ever, you're a cheaper thrill.
How can this be? Abuse compels
a lover
to desire more but admire less.

73

THE UGLY TRUTH

Stop wanting to be thanked by anyone
anywhere; stop thinking anyone is honorable.
Ingratitude is ubiquitous: there's no profit
in kindness, only a tedious bother.
In fact, no one has hurt me more gravely
than my one true friend.

74

UNCLE HARPOCRATES

Gellius heard that his uncle disdained
love-making and love-talk.
As a precaution he stuck it to his aunt,
and his uncle said nothing. Now he does
what he wants, for although his uncle
is screwed, he never says a word.

75

EXHAUSTION

My opinion of you is laid low, Lesbia,
tua culpa. I am spent:
I couldn't respect you at your best
nor quit you for any offense.

76

ENTREATY

Catullus, if men take pleasure in
recalling good deeds or times when
they were decent, broke no promises,
deceived no one by violating sacred oaths,
then great joy awaits after this thankless affair.
Whatever men say or do well, you have said
and done. Whatever you invested –
your return was nothing. Why punish
yourself further? Can't you pull
yourself together, snap out of it, stop   10
wallowing in misery? It's hard to
put aside love, hard, but you must.
This is your one salvation: you
must overcome, and you will, able
or unable. Gods, if there is pity in heaven,
if you ever save mortals in danger,
notice me: if I have lived well,
lift from me this ruinous plague,
this torpor dragging my limbs, reaching
up to wrench the joy from my heart.   20
I won't ask that she love me or,
since it's impossible, that she be chaste.
I just want to be well, free from depressive
disgrace. Please, gods, pay back my piety.

77

THIEF

Rufus, my friend trusted in vain
(in vain and at great price),
did you really steal from me,
burn me, snatch every joy
I had? Goddamn it, you did:
you're poison to me,
plague to friendship.

78

ALL IN THE FAMILY I

✥

Oh, about Gallus' brothers, one has
a charming wife, one a delicious son.
Gallus is a darling:
he orchestrates their affair.
Gallus is a fool:
he doesn't see the irony of teaching
his nephew to cuckold his uncle.

78b

SPOILED

Sadly, your rank saliva pissed on the
pristine lips of a lovely girl.
You won't get away with it: future
ages will know you as a famous old whore.

79

HER BROTHER

Lesbius is gorgeous, and why not? –
She prefers him to you and yours, Catullus.
But that hunk would sell his family and yours
for three willing mouths among friends.

80

THE EVIDENCE

What shall I say, Gellius? Why
are your rosy lips whiter than frost
when you leave home in the morning,
when you wake from summer's
soft siesta? I don't know for sure,
but rumor has it that you crave
a certain swelling. This much is certain:
the bulging balls of your victim spill
the news, the evidence still on your lips.

81

SLUMMING

🙥🙥

Was there no one else to crave, Juventius,
no other sugar daddy in all of Rome
but that jaundiced stranger dredged up
from some Umbrian backwater,
whom now you adore, even prefer to me,
somehow unconscious of your crime?

82

ALL EYES

Quintius, if you want me to owe you
my eyes or something even more precious,
don't take from me what is far dearer
than eyes or anything dearer than that.

83

HER HUSBAND

When her husband's around, Lesbia
insults me viciously:
for that dupe there's no greater pleasure.
Fool, don't you get it? If she had forgotten
me, she would be silent —
that would make sense:
when she snarls and growls,
not only
does she remember, but what's hotter,
she's on fire: when she burns, she talks.   10

84

PUTTING ON HAIRS

Arrius kept saying "hopportune" when he meant
"opportune," "hinsidious" for "insidious."
And he was so henamoured of this mode
that he himself became hunbearable.
His mother, his upstart uncle, his
maternal grandparents probably spoke
this way. When he was in Syria,
our ears got some relief: they heard
the same words but with smoother
breathing; they began to have faith in the future   10
till a horrible herald was hannounced:
the Ionian Sea, following Harrius' journey,
was hafterwards called "Hionian."

85

ODETAMO

I hate and I love.
Perhaps you wonder why.
I don't know, but I feel it, and I am crucified.

86

ON BEAUTY

To many, Quintia's a beauty.
She's fair, tall, and built: these I confess,
but "beauty" I deny: there's no charm,
no bite of spice in that tall drink.
Beauty is Lesbia, singular, superlative:
she alone snatched the very salt from Venus.

87

CONTRACT

No woman will be loved as Lesbia was by me,
no faith in any oath as fierce as my love for you.

88

ALL IN THE FAMILY II

※

Who is it, Gellius, who scratches his itch
on his mother and sister, watches
over their nudity? Who's making himself
his aunt's husband? Do you know what
a crime he commits? One neither far
Tethys nor Ocean, father of nymphs, could
wash clean. There's nothing worse he could do,
not even if he sucked his own dick.

89

ALL IN THE FAMILY III

Gellius is thin, and why not?
How could he not be lean
with such a vibrant mother,
so charming a sister, so obliging
an uncle, and so many girls
for relations? If he never touched
any but those related to him, you'd
still find him thin as you pleased.

90

THE PERSIAN PRIESTHOOD

May a magus be born
from the unspeakable union
of Gellius and his mother
(fitting offspring of mother and son
if there's truth to rumors
of Persian religion), and may
he study Persian soothsaying
and honor the gods with familiar song,
melting fatty innards in the flame.

91

ANY AVAILABLE CRIME

I knew I couldn't trust you, Gellius,
when I lost my love: I knew you well,
never found you constant, able to restrain
your filthy ways. But my love was neither
mother nor sister to you: we were familiar,
but I didn't think that cause enough:
Was I wrong! What joy you take in
every vice, in any available crime.

92

LYING

Lesbia's always a bitch,
never shuts up about me:
I swear she loves me.
Why? I'm just the same:
I curse her up and down,
but I'd die without her.

93

BRUSH OFF

✻

I'm not very eager to please you, Caesar,
nor to know what breed you are.

94

THE ADVENTURES OF LITTLE PRICK I

Little Prick fucks around. He fucks around? Of course.
It's like they say: the jar chooses its own pickles.

95ab

CINNA'S EPIC REDUCTION

After nine harvests, nine winters' labor,
Cinna has finally birthed his "Zmyrna."
Hortensius, meanwhile, spewed
half a million lines ...
"Zmyrna"'s deep fame will outlast generations,
outspread the river it celebrates,
while Volusius' pages languish,
damp wrapping for mackerel
in the shallows of the Po ...
... the annals of my heart are small ...   10
let the horde have tumid Antimachus.

96

LEGACY

※

If some part of grief falls welcome
at the feet of the silent dead,
if desire renews old love
and weeping friendship lost,
then Quintilia finds more joy in
love than pain in her early death.

97

ALL KINDS OF ASS

※

I swear you can't tell Aemilius'
mouth from his asshole. The
former's not at all clean, the
latter's equally filthy. Really,
his ass is preferable: it has no teeth.
His mouth boasts long tusks
caressed by rawhide gums;
it has the gaping look of a mule cunt
pissing a seething spray. He fucks
plenty of women, thinks himself charming: 10
he should be mucking out donkey stalls.
Whoever touched that man must be able
to tongue the ass of a diseased meat-grinder.

98

BAD BREATH

Stinking Victus, if anyone can be
called a fatuous blowhard, it's you.
When opportunity knocks,
you'd lick out assholes and lug soles.
If you want to slay us, Victus,
exhale: you'll get your wish.

99

TORURE

Juventius, my sweet, while you were playing
I stole a kiss more tempting than ambrosia.
Not that I wasn't punished:
I recall being nailed to your cross
for more than an hour, unable to slip free
or buy with tears respite from your wrath:
you scrubbed your lips with droplets
from your delicate fingers
lest there remain any trace of my taste,
sour as a pissed-on whore.   10
All the while you kept delivering me
to Eros, torturing me by every means
till that little kiss became
more biting than bitter hellebore.
Since you exact such punishment
from your tormented love, never
will I steal another kiss.

100

BROTHERLY LOVE (AUFILLENA I)

Caelius and Quintius, flowers of Verona,
want Aufillenus and Aufillena.
One wants the brother, the other the sister.
Now that's what I call brotherly love!
Whom would I back? You, Caelius:
your singular friendship came clear to me
when a needling flame licked my bones.
May you be lucky, Caelius, lucky in love.

101

AVE ATQUE VALE

Dear brother,
Over seas and through many lands
I come to your funeral rites
to give one final gift, to address
in vain your silent ashes.
Fortune stole you from me,
rent you from me too soon. And so,
tradition at my back, I attend
to ritual and offer this last gift:
take it with my tears, and forever,   10
brother, be well and farewell.

102

SHHH ...

If anyone can be trusted to silence
by a faithful friend whose stainless soul
is known deeply, consider me,
Cornelius, bound by sacred oath;
consider me Harpocrates himself.

103

A PROPER PIMP

If you please, sir, return my payment;
then be as savage and rude as you like.
Or, if you prefer, pray stop being a pimp;
then be as savage and rude as you like.

104

THE LAST WORD ON LESBIA

You think I could say anything bad
about my love, my life, the one dearer
than my eyes? I can't. If I could,
I wouldn't love with such abandon:
you make a farce out of everything!

105

THE ADVENTURES OF LITTLE PRICK II

Little Prick tried to climb their sacred mount:
the Muses caught the tool and tossed him out.

106

FOR SALE?

When you see a dealer with a beautiful boy,
don't you assume he wants to sell?

107

SWEET RELIEF

Whenever something hopeful
befalls a hopeless soul,
it's welcome relief. And
it is a welcome relief
more precious than gold that
you returned to me, Lesbia:
you came back to my desire
and my hope. What a splendid day!
Who alive is luckier? Whose
life is more blessed than mine?   10

108

COMINIUS: DOTAGE DISMEMBERED

If your disgraceful dotage, hoary
and tarnished, met its end at the hands
of the people, surely your evil tongue
would be first to go, ripped from
its roots by a vulture; a raven would
gorge on your pecked-out eyes, dogs
eat your innards, wolves your limbs.

LEGALESE

You promise that our love will never die.
Dear god, let this be true:
make her vow sincere and from the heart,
let this eternal pact, this sweet allegiance, rule our lives.

110

COMPARISON SHOPPING (AUFILLENA II)

Good whores, Aufillena, are valuable
goods: they earn the fee they arrange.
To do what you promise is noble,
to promise not at all, chaste. You promise,
but you lie, take but won't give it up:
you're like a fraudulent whore, snatching
back favors; you're worse than a profitrix,
selling each crevice and inch.

III

ALL IN THE FAMILY IV (AUFILLENA III)

To live and die with one man,
Aufillena, is the pride of every bride,
but better to sleep with anyone
than beget brothers by an uncle.

112

UNKNOWN NASO

※

You're a lot of man, Naso:
no man would go down with you,
but you'd go down on anyone.

113

BY THE NUMBERS

In Pompey's first consulship, Cinna,
two men enjoyed Maecilia:
in the second, the same two remained,
enlarged by a thousand degrees:
seed loves well-tilled soil.

THE ADVENTURES OF LITTLE PRICK III

They say Little Prick's estate is blessed
with endless bounty: every clucking bird,
meadows and fields, fish and game – all in vain.
Expenditures eat up the yield. I'll admit he's
rich provided he's a pauper, praise
the estate whose master's in great need.

115

THE ADVENTURES OF LITTLE PRICK IV

Little Prick's got twenty acres for flock,
another thirty to plow: then there's the swamp.
You'd think he'd rival Croesus,
such wealth in a single plot:
meadowlands, forests deep, and
swampy expanse from here to the Northern
Lights, there to the edge of the world.
All this impresses, but Little Prick himself is
best: no mere man but grand imposing tool.

ARCHERY

When still inclined to want you,
I tempted you with poems
of sacred Battus, tried to soften
your view, reduce the arsenal
aimed at my head. Now I see
this was in vain, Gellius:
my prayers have failed.
I'll evade your attack, and you'll pay
the penalty, fixed in my own sights.

Notes

General: Please recall that all titles are our own: Catullus, following the poetic conventions of his time, did not title individual poems. Our translations are based on Kenneth Quinn's (1973)[1] edition of Catullus' Latin, and we rely on his excellent notes as well as his wisdom in accepting standard emendations of the Latin manuscripts.

We take liberty with the names of Greek and Roman gods and goddesses, using, for example, the names Zeus, Jupiter, and Jove interchangeably. In his poetry Catullus pays homage to his Greek predecessors, whose influence he acknowledges. Our occasional use of Greek names for Roman deities, therefore, reflects Catullus' debt to poets like Sappho and Callimachus in addition to offering the most liberal scope of possibility for translation and the greatest potential for accessibility to a modern audience.

Where we feel our translation is a reasonably accurate and clear interpretation of Catullus' Latin for a reader of modern English, we have said little by way of annotation. Where our reading has foreclosed other crucial readings of the Latin, where manuscript difficulties occasion multiple and/or problematic readings, or where the names of persons, mythological material, or geographical names may be opaque, we offer notes below. We do not repeat notes; that is, once we have identified a person or place, we do not redefine that person or place in every subsequent poem in which he/she/it appears.

In his corpus, Catullus refers to and addresses many people by name, many of whom are unattested elsewhere and therefore unknown to us as historical figures. Were these real people? Were they Catullus' friends and fellow poets, orators or politicians contemporary with Catullus? Often the speaker's tone leads us to answer in the affirmative, and there has been ample speculation as to the historical identity of Catullus' cast of characters; however, we have been cautious not to assume too much about names in a text, and we do not slip easily into the assumption that Catullus' poetry is

---

[1] Kenneth Quinn, *Catullus: The Poems* (St. Martin's Press, 1973).

necessarily autobiographical. Where wide scholarly agreement exists as to the historical identity of a person named in the corpus, we offer it, but we do not engage in speculation in the absence of clear and compelling evidence. In certain cases where a proper name does not contribute to the sense of the poem and is otherwise unknown, we omit it from the translation altogether and relegate it to the notes.

Our line numbers count only lines of text and ellipses, not lines intentionally left blank. Many ancient poems come down to the modern period as fragments or with lines missing; ellipses in our translations stand for lines of Latin text lost in transmission.

I DEDICATION

We offer copious notes on Catullus' dedicatory poem because it is crucial to our understanding and interpretation of the corpus. Elsewhere we will not delve quite so deeply into issues of manuscript tradition and emendation. For more information, see pp. 1–6.

3 Cornelius Nepos was a well-known Roman historian and biographer, a contemporary of Catullus.

5 Classicists do not agree as to Catullus' tone here. This poem sets Catullus' genre apart from that of his dedicatee, but whether the *doctis* and *laboriosis* used to describe Nepos' works are complimentary or pejorative is unclear. Was Catullus dedicating his collection to Cornelius Nepos in a tone of earnest respect? Was he ribbing his dedicatee for undertaking such grandiose topics but writing only three scrolls? Or did Catullus, in fact, view Nepos' work with some disdain? Our translation sits somewhere between the second and third possibilities and intends to highlight not only Catullus' generic consciousness but also his penchant for literary critique. We take inspiration from the way in which Sappho, Callimachus, and their respective contemporaries distinguish their genres from the genres of their predecessors, sometimes expressing apparent disdain for other literary modes while also at times borrowing from them.

8 In part because of a tricky manuscript issue at the end of this poem (which has occasioned multiple emendations and much scholarly debate), but also because of the apparent double-dedication within the poem, the gender and identity of the recipient of the direct address in the penultimate line of the Latin are in dispute. Catullus here either refers back to Cornelius Nepos, calling him his patron, or he addresses someone he calls *patrona virgo*,

perhaps a Muse or goddess: in Latin *virgo* means maiden or virgin. We take the more standard reading, translating *patrona virgo* as "dear Muse." For an overview and history of the debate, see A. S. Gratwick, "*Vale, Patrona Virgo*: The Text of Catullus 1.9," *Classical Quarterly* 52.1 (2002: 305–320), keeping in mind that we do not follow Gratwick's proposed emendation here.

2AB ATALANTA

This poem combines what may be two. poetic fragments. Some scholars consider them part of the same whole; others take them as two separate poems; in Latin editions these are known either as poem 2 or as 2a (our lines 1–7) and 2b (8–10). There is no break in the manuscripts, but a suggestion in the Renaissance that the poem comprised two different fragments changed the way the poem was considered and continues to influence scholars today. Martin and Green both translate 2ab as two separate poems, Martin calling them 1b and 2.

9 The "nimble maiden" is Atalanta, a well-known huntress from Greek and Roman mythology, who wished to remain a virgin forever and therefore challenged every suitor to a footrace for her hand. She won each race until her final suitor, with the help of Aphrodite (whose Roman counterpart is Venus), distracted Atalanta by throwing golden apples into her path, won the race, and became her husband.

3 DIRGE

1 Venus is the Roman goddess of love and desire and mother of Aeneas, one of the mythical founders of Rome; Cupid is Venus' son and a god of love and desire in his own right.

14 Orcus is a Roman god of the Underworld whose origins may be Etruscan; in Roman mythology, the Underworld itself could also be known as Orcus.

4 PERSONIFICATION

1 The pirogue is not a Mediterranean vessel, but we use it here to recall its use in Derek Walcott's *Omeros*, giving a nod not only to that poem but to the many ways in which ancient Greek and Roman culture is translated for a modern audience.

7 Marmara is a region on the Black Sea in what is now northwestern Turkey.

7 Thracian refers to Thrace, a region adjacent to Marmara on the Black Sea in what is now southeastern Bulgaria, northeastern Greece, and north-western Turkey.

8 Pontic refers to the Black Sea, as in line 12.

11 Cytorian refers to the city of Cytorus on the Black Sea; we omit in our translation the name of a similar port city, Amastris (Latin line 13), but we address other "Cities of the Black Sea" in line 12.

19 Jupiter is a sky god, the father and political head of the Roman pantheon, Roman counterpart of the Greek Zeus.

21 *terra firma* is a Latin phrase often used untranslated in English. It means literally "hard or firm earth or land" and is often synonymous with "dry land."

23 Castor and Pollux are brothers – twin children of Leda – but their divinity is imperfect since one of the twins is said to have been fathered by the mortal Tyndareus and the other by Zeus, and in their mythology they seem to split one share of immortality. The pair often lends help to human beings, particularly to sailors.

5 TIME AND NUMBER

1 The name Lesbia appears throughout the corpus; on Lesbia, see pp. 16–30.

11 The implication here is that knowledge of specific information like numbers opens the couple to the danger of being cursed by observers.

6 KISS AND TELL

1 The name Flavius appears only here, and we cannot identify an historical Flavius with certainty.

7 KISSINGS OF YOU

Title The title of this poem attempts to translate *basiationes*, a Latin word apparently coined by Catullus, which appears in the first line of the poem and is something equivalent to "kissifications."

3 Cyrene was a city in what is now northern Libya and birthplace of the Hellenistic poet Callimachus.

4 Silphium is a plant native to Cyrene (its main export in the Roman period) used for a variety of culinary and medical purposes including perhaps contraception.

5 Jove is another name for Jupiter.

6 Battus was the first king of the Greek colony whose capital was Cyrene, and his name in Catullus is read as a reference to the poet Callimachus.

13 As in poem 5, we see here attention to knowledge of numbers and the fear of being cursed.

8 IT'S OVER

20 The Latin we have translated "be a man" says literally "be hard, persist."

9 ADVENTUS

Title *Adventus* means "arrival" in Latin; the *adventus* of the emperor was a stock scene in Roman historical relief.

1 The name Veranius also appears in poems 12, 28, and 47; a Veranius may have served in Spain as Catullus did in Bithynia, assuming this aspect of Catullus' corpus is autobiographical, as most scholars believe it is.

10 THE WHORE

1 The name Varus also appears in poem 22; Varus may be the lawyer Alfenus Varus or Quintilius Varus, friend of Horace and Vergil (Quinn, *Catullus*, 121).

1 The Roman Forum was the heart of the city and the locus of Roman business, *negotium* in Latin. The fact that Catullus' speaker is at leisure (*otiosum*) in the locus of *negotium* says something significant about his place in the socio-economic fabric of the city: he is out of place. Notice that in Latin business is literally the negation (*negare*, "to deny") of leisure (*otium*), and of course *negotium* gives us the English cognate "negotiate." See also p. 13.

6 Bithynia was a Roman province in what is now northwest Turkey where the speaker claims to have served under the governor Memmius.

14 Properly speaking, the governor is called *irrumator*, "mouth-fuck," not "butt-fuck," but since the two verbs are used as a pair in poem 16, we opted here for the term more common in modern English.

24 Serapis was an Egyptian god whose cult gained popularity in Rome during Catullus' lifetime.

26 This line may refer to the poet Gaius Helvius Cinna of poem 95ab, whom Catullus clearly respects a great deal, and/or to the Cinna of poem 113. In the narrative of poem 10, Varus' unsophisticated girlfriend has ironically caught the speaker in a lie, and Catullus seems to mix up the names here in order to show his speaker struggling nervously to explain.

11 MESSAGE TO MY LOVE

1 The name Furius also appears in poems 16, 23, and 26; he may be the poet M. Furius Bibaculus. See pp. 11–12.

1 The name Aurelius also appears in poems 15, 16, and 21, but we cannot identify an historical Aurelius with certainty.

3 Aurora is the Roman goddess of dawn.

4 The people we call "Persian" Catullus calls Hyrcanian in reference to Hyrcania, a region south of the Caspian Sea in what is now part of Iran and Turkmenistan.

5 Scythian refers to a large and diverse region to the north and east of what is now western Europe, some of which borders on the Black Sea.

5 Parthian refers to a region in what is now northeastern Iran.

7 Here and throughout the corpus Caesar is Gaius Julius Caesar, member of the so-called First Triumvirate, later named dictator for life after defeating Pompey and crossing the Rubicon into Rome; Caesar was assassinated in 44 BC.

8 Gallic refers to a region comprising what is now primarily France.

8 Brits refers to the peoples of Roman Britain, characterized here as inhabiting the westernmost border of Rome's territory.

12 NAPKIN THIEF

1 Asinius' full name is Asinius Marrucinus.

8 We have omitted the name of Asinius' brother, Pollio, who, according to Quinn, was Gaius Asinius Pollio, orator and historian, and friend of Horace and Vergil.[2]

15 We have omitted the geographical name Saetabis, a Spanish city famous for linens in Catullus' time.

17 The name Fabullus appears again in poems 13, 28, and 47, but he is otherwise unknown.

17 This may be the Veranius named in poems 9, 28 and 47.

---

[2] Quinn, *Catullus*, 131

13 BYOB

Title This is the title given to poem 13 in *Wheelock's Latin*, but it is too perfect not to use it again here.

2 The name Fabullus also appears in poems 12, 28, and 47.

14 THE GIFT

1 Calvus also appears in poem 53 in which he plays the roles of orator and poet; he is probably C. Licinius Macer Calvus, who is probably also the Licinius of poem 50.

2 P. Vatinius, a skillful and apparently unscrupulous politician, also appears in poems 52 and 53, in which Calvus speaks publicly against him. See Quinn, who calls Vatinius "the best-hated man of his time" (Quinn, *Catullus*, 246).

8 Sulla is perhaps a freedman of the famous Roman dictator Lucius Cornelius Sulla (Felix), but the specific reference here is unclear. See Quinn, *Catullus*, 137–8.

13 Saturnalia is the Roman holiday falling nearest the winter solstice, a time for gift-giving, general festivity, and the inversion of social norms.

16 The name Caesius appears only here, and Caesius is otherwise unknown.

16 Aquinus appears only here and cannot be identified with certainty, but an Aquinius is mentioned by Cicero (*Tusc.* 5.63): see Quinn, *Catullus*, 138.

16 The name Suffenus appears again in poem 22, but Suffenus is otherwise unknown.

14B INTRODUCTORY FRAGMENT

In the manuscripts, this poem follows 14 without a break, but it appears to be incomplete as transmitted.

15 THIS ONE BOY

1 The name Aurelius also appears in poems 11, 16, and 21.

16 PERSONA

1 If our interpretation is correct, these are the Furius and Aurelius of poem 11: see p. 185.

17 HOMETOWN HERO

1 The first line of the poem is corrupt and restored from line 7 of the Latin poem, which names a *Colonia*. It is unclear whether Catullus intended to refer here to Verona or to a more general *colonia*, a colonial town or settlement; scholars agree that Catullus hailed from Verona, a fact referenced again in poem 67.

6 Line 6 of the Latin poem seems to refer to an unknown ritual of some sort called the Salisubsalus (or perhaps to a god of the same name). It is fun — and, to my mind, consistent with the tone of the poem — to imagine that this word could be a joke or pun, something lost on modern readers. Whatever the case, we omit the specific reference and instead invoke the singing of songs as a general indication of communal ritual.

20 Ligurian refers to a northwestern coastal region of Italy.

18–20

The manuscripts jump from poem 17 to poem 21, reflecting the removal from the corpus of three poems (now agreed not to have been written by Catullus) that had been added by Muret in a 1554 edition.

21 THIS ONE BOY II

This poem is a return to the addressee and theme of poem 15.

22 OUR BACKPACKS

1 The name Suffenus also appears in poem 14.

2 The name Varus also appears in poem 10.

23 DRY AND CRISP

2 This may be the Furius of poems 11, 16, and 26.

24 JUVENTIUS

2 Juventius also appears in poems 48, 81, and 99. He cannot be identified with any specific historical figure, but a family of Juventii is attested at Rome at this time. Juventius may also be the boy of poems 15 and 21. In Latin, the word *juventus* means simply "youth."

4 Midas was a mythical king of Phrygia (in what is now central Turkey) who wished that everything he touched might turn to gold. Once granted, this gift quickly proved a curse when he could not eat or drink or touch his loved ones.

25 THREAT

1 Thallus appears only here and is otherwise unknown.
5 Manuscripts vary on this line; we accept Quinn's edition and translate the Latin *diva Murcia* as Sloth.

26 ENCUMBERED

1 This may be the Furius of poems 11, 16, and 23.

27 SYMPOSIUM

3 Falernian was one of the most famous and well-regarded wines produced in Catullus' time.
4 Postumia is the mistress of ceremonies in the poem. She is otherwise unknown, but a Postumius appears in poem 67, and the two may be siblings based on what we know of Roman naming conventions. In Latin, *postumus* (the superlative of *posterus*) means "final" or "last," but Postumus is also a common Latin surname and Postumius the name of a Roman family.
7 Bacchus is the Roman god of wine, Roman counterpart of the Greek god Dionysus, used here, as often in Latin, to stand for wine itself.

28 IN SERVICE

1 Most agree that Piso is a reference to L. Calpurnius Piso Caesoninus, who was a provincial governor at the time, but as Quinn notes, Veranius and Fabullus are said to have been in Spain in poem 12, whereas Piso was governor of Macedonia (Quinn, *Catullus*, 172–3). The name Piso also appears in poem 47.
3 This may be the Veranius of poems 9, 12, and 47.
4 This may be the Fabullus of poems 12, 13, and 47.
8 Memmius was the governor of Bithynia during the speaker's service. While Memmius is not named in poem 10, Catullus does refer there to the *irrumator praetor* of Bithynia, which we translate "butt-fuck governor" in 10.14. This must be the same Memmius.

15   The Latin text specifically names Romulus and Remus, twin brothers and mythical founders of Rome. Our translation offers a more general nod to Roman tradition (and Rome's founding fathers) with the phrase *mos maiorum*, sometimes used untranslated in English, which means literally "the customs or habits of those greater" or "the ways of the ancestors."

29   THE SPENDTHRIFT

3   Mamurra also appears in poem 57 and was a well-known historical figure who made his fortune serving in the foreign campaigns of Caesar and Pompey. Scholars speculate that in poems 94, 105, 114, and 115 the name Mentula (which we translate "Little Prick") is a pseudonym for Mamurra: the Latin *mentula* appears in this poem in line 15, where we translate it "little prick" for consistency.

9   Adonis is a mythological figure known for his unparalleled beauty, an object of both Aphrodite's and Persephone's affections. He is sometimes called a god of beauty, but in mythology his immortality is problematic; probably as a result of this ambiguity, Adonis was worshiped in mystery religions, whose focus was often the cycle of death and rebirth.

21   Here we omit the name of the gold-bearing Spanish river Tagus, which is given in the Latin.

25   Pompey here and elsewhere in the corpus is Gnaeus Pompeius Magnus, Pompey the Great, member of the so-called First Triumvirate along with Gaius Julius Caesar and Marcus Licinius Crassus, and son-in-law of Caesar, assassinated in Egypt in 48 BC after being defeated in the Battle of Pharsalus.

30   FORGETFUL

1   If Alfenus is the lawyer Alfenus Varus, then the Alfenus of poem 30 could also be the Varus of poems 10 and 22.

31   NOSTOS

Title *Nostos* means "homecoming" in ancient Greek and is used to refer to homecomings like that of Odysseus. The word gives us one morpheme of the two that make up the word nostalgia in English. The other, *algos*, means "pain."

1 Sirmio is a peninsula at the southern end of Lake Garda near Verona.

3 Neptune is the Roman god of the sea, Roman counterpart of the Greek Poseidon.

7 Catullus jokes here that if there is a Bithynia, there must also be a Thynia (where bi- is a prefix meaning two), and he draws out the joke by making the adjective plural (*Bithynos*), suggesting that he may be talking about the Bithynian people until the following line, where the reader finds that Catullus is referring to "Thynia and the Bithynian fields" (*campos*), a "single" Thynia implied from the "double" Bi-thynia. This is a little like saying in English that if there is a Bismark (a Bi-smark), there must also be a Smark. Catullus does use the Latin adjective Thynus (rather than Bithynus) in poem 25 (*catagraphosque Thynos*), and Thyni is attested in the Greek historian Herodotus, but Roman authors seem to use the names interchangeably, allowing the joke to hold.

16 While Catullus calls the lake Lydian (in Latin *Lydiae*), he does so because the Etruscans who inhabited Italy were thought to have come from Lydia in what is now Turkey.

32 SWEET IPSITILLA

1 Nothing is known of Ipsitilla: the name is otherwise unattested and looks like a possible conflation of two Latin pronouns meaning "she herself" and "that girl" (*ipsa et illa*). It may otherwise be a double diminutive of *ipsa*.

33 FAMILY BUSINESS

1 The name Vibennius appears only here, and Vibennius is otherwise unknown.

1 This is a play on the standard "Vibennius and Son."

34 DIANA'S SONG

1 Diana is the Roman goddess of the moon, the hunt, and childbirth. A perpetual virgin herself, she is associated with forests and wild animals.

4 We have repeated the final line of this stanza at the end of every stanza to convey the hymnic quality of the poem.

5 Latona is Diana's mother, making Diana's matronymic Latonia.

6 Zeus is the sky god and king of the Greek pantheon; the Latin here says "King Jupiter."

13 Juno Lucina is a Roman goddess of childbirth, one of the aspects of the goddess Juno.

14 Trivia is the Roman goddess of the crossroads, also associated with the moon, death, and witchcraft like her Greek counterpart, Hecate.

35 UNFINISHED

1 Caecilius is an unknown figure, apparently a poet; the name Caecilius appears again in poem 67.

11 "Cybele" refers to an unfinished poetic work by Caecilius. In the Latin, Catullus refers to this work as the *Magna Mater* ("Great Mother") and also as the *Dindymi dominam* ("Mistress of Dindymus"), all references to the goddess Cybele whose cult is the subject not only of Caecilius' unfinished poem but also of Catullus' poem 63.

14 Sappho's Muse could be Aphrodite, or Catullus might intend his audience to think generally here about Sappho's inspiration; the point might even be that Sappho and her poetry function as a Muse: Sappho was called the tenth Muse by Plato. The original nine Muses were Greek goddesses thought to offer inspiration to those engaged in a variety of creative and academic pursuits: particularly what we think of now as the fine arts, but also history and astronomy.

36 INTO THE FIRE

1 Volusius is an otherwise unknown poet who appears to have written a work called the *Annals*. The name appears again in poem 95ab.

11 Aphrodite is the Greek goddess of love and desire.

11 Idalion was an ancient city in Cyprus sacred to Aphrodite/Venus, as were all the cities named below.

12 Urion was a city in Apulia.

13 Ancon (or Ancona) was a city on the Adriatic Sea northeast of Rome.

13 Knidos was an ancient Greek city in Caria, modern southwestern Turkey.

13 Amathos was a city in Cyprus.

13 Golgi was a city in Cyprus.

14 Dyrrachion was a port city on the coast of Illyria opposite what is now Brindisi.

37 CATHOUSE TAVERN

15 An Egnatius also appears in poem 39, and while scholars speculate, there is no clear evidence as to his historical identity.

38 CONSOLATION

1 Cornificius may be Quintus Cornificius, an orator, poet, and contemporary of Catullus who served under Caesar during the Civil Wars (Quinn, *Catullus*, 206; Chester L. Neudling, *A Prosopography to Catullus* (Iowa Studies in Classical Philology 12; Oxford, 1955): 52–57).

39 DR. TEETH

1 This is the Egnatius of poem 37, as we can tell by the teeth/urine connection.

11 Sabine refers to an ancient region of Italy encompassing the central Apennines and Latium north of the Anio River.

12 Tiburtine refers to an ancient region of Italy around modern Tivoli in Lazio.

12 Etruscan refers to an ancient region of Italy encompassing Tuscany, western Umbria, and northern Latium.

13 Lanuvian refers to the ancient city Lanuvium in Latium (modern Lanuvio).

14 Transpadane refers to a region north of the Po River known in the Roman period as Cisalpine Gaul.

40 IMPALED

1 The name Ravidus appears only here and cannot be identified with any historical figure.

41 FORMIANUS' GIRLFRIEND I

Title Ameana is called *amica Formiani* ("girlfriend of the man from Formiae") in line 4 of the Latin poem; we omit this name from the body of the poem but retain the identification in the title. If we can trust Horace and Catullus that Mamurra was from Formiae (Catullus says as much in poem 57), then Ameana is probably the girlfriend of Mamurra, who is here given the pseudonym Formianus, "the man from Formiae."

1 The name Ameana appears only once in the corpus and is otherwise unknown; however, Ameana is clearly the subject of poem 43 too, hence our title.

44 AT TIVOLI

8 Sestius is Publius Sestius, a well-known political figure in Catullus' time. Catullus' assessment of him here is echoed by Cicero (*Fam.* 7.32.1). See Quinn, *Catullus,* 222.

9 Antius appears only here and cannot be securely identified; he may be the C. Antius Restio who supported sumptuary legislation meant to limit expenditure on dinner parties (Macrob. 3.17.13, Gell. 2.24.13).

45 ACME AND SEPTIMIUS

An unknown couple.

46 LEAVING BITHYNIA

3 Zephyr (Zephyrus) is the mythological name of the west wind.
5 Nicaea was a city in Bithynia.

47 PASSED OVER

1 Porcius appears only here and is an unknown figure whose name is cognate with the Latin word for pig; Socration, diminutive of the name Socrates, may be the Epicurean philosopher Philodemus, who may have gone with Piso to Macedonia, but the suggestion is speculative (Quinn, *Catullus,* 231). These two colorful names are likely to have been used here as pseudonyms.

48 INSATIABLE

1 This is the Juventius of poems 24, 81, and 99.

49 CICERO

1 Marcus Tullius Cicero was a well-known orator, politician, and philosopher during Catullus' lifetime; he was politically conservative, a supporter of the Senate and the traditional Roman Republic during the civil wars.

His attitude toward Catullus' poetic circle is discussed briefly in the introduction to this volume, pp. 3–4.

50 EROTICA

1 Licinius is probably C. Licinius Macer Calvus, a poet contemporary with Catullus, and perhaps also the Calvus of poems 14 and 53; if so, he is addressed as Licinius only in poem 50.
14 Nemesis is the Greek goddess of revenge and retribution.

51 SAPPHO'S POEM/GET A JOB

As its name implies, this poem is at least in part a translation of Sappho's poem 31 (*phainetai moi*). The fourth and final stanza of Catullus' version is much debated because it diverges significantly from Sappho's fourth stanza, leading some scholars to speculate that Catullus' final stanza was part of a different poem. Our interpretation acknowledges the difference between Catullus' version and Sappho's original while asserting the unity of Catullus' poem as a whole. *Get a Job* is the "title" of our translation of Catullus' fourth stanza; Sappho's fourth stanza continues the bodily imagery of her previous three stanzas, culminating in a description of lovesickness, death, or perhaps orgasm. Following Sappho's fourth stanza, one fragmentary line remains. See Diane Rayor's 2014 translation of Sappho's Greek below. In addition, line 8 of the Latin poem is missing from our manuscripts of Catullus.

Sappho [31]

To me it seems that man has the fortune
 of gods, whoever sits beside you
and close, who listens to you
sweetly speaking

and laughing temptingly. My heart
flutters in my breast whenever
I even glance at you –
I can say nothing,
my tongue is broken. A delicate fire

10   runs under my skin, my eyes
      see nothing, my ears roar,
      cold sweat

      rushes down me, trembling seizes me,
      I am greener than grass.
      To myself I seem
      needing but little to die.

52 CORRUPTION

2 Nonius is difficult to identify with certainty.
2 The curule chair was the seat and symbol of the highest order of political and military power in Rome.
3 This seems to be the Vatinius of poems 14 and 53.

54 TURN OFFS

None of the figures in this poem can be identified with certainty, although Libo may be L. Scribonius Libo, supporter of Pompey the Great until Pompey's defeat at Pharsalus. In addition, there are a number of manuscript difficulties with the poem. The manuscripts are corrupt in line 2 of the Latin, and thus the name Hirrus is speculative. After the first line of poem 54, lines 16–17 of poem 50 are repeated. The manuscripts read Sufficio rather than Fufidio in line 5. Fufidio was suggested by Bickel (1949) because of the appearance of a fellow named Fufidius in a satire of Horace (1.2.12–17) and because the name Sufficius is otherwise unknown and thought to be corrupt. See Quinn, *Catullus*, 249–50.

55 HIDEOUT

3 The Campus Minor is otherwise unattested, a geographical reference lost on the modern reader but certainly somewhere in the city of Rome.
3–4 The Circus Maximus was an ancient stadium located in the city of Rome between the Palatine and Aventine hills.
5 The Temple of Jove was located on the Capitoline Hill in Rome.
8 The name Camerius appears again in poem 58b, which may originally have been part of poem 55; in fact, lines 9–12 of poem 55 are corrupt in

the manuscripts, perhaps indicating that poem 58b at one point resided somewhere within it: some late manuscripts even insert 58b into poem 55. While a translation following these combinations is, on the one hand, compelling, it is commonplace in the manuscripts for poems on the same topic to be separated from one another. Witness poems 41 and 43, for example, or the Little Prick series at the end of the corpus.

8 Identifications of an historical Camerius are speculative.

12 Heracles is a Greek mythological figure famous for his divine parentage, his godlike strength and hyper-masculinity, and the twelve labors that eventually won him his place in the pantheon.

56 LAUGHABLE

1 Cato is probably the poet P. Valerius Cato, although from the tone of poem 56, this Cato could easily have been confused with the conservative prude M. Porcius Cato, famous for having opposed Julius Caesar.

58 THAT LESBIA

1 As Quinn puts it, "it is both tempting and plausible" to identify Caelius as M. Caelius Rufus (Quinn, *Catullus,* 258), the man who became Clodia's lover after Catullus, assuming Lesbia is Clodia Metelli. Of course, all this relies on an autobiographical reading of the corpus. Some argue that the Caelius of poem 58 is also the Rufus of poems 69 and 77. A Caelius also appears in poem 100.

58B CAMERIUS II

1 Talos was a bronze giant crafted to be watchman on the island of Crete either for the protection of Minos or Europa.

2 Pegasus was a mythological winged, white horse, offspring of Poseidon.

3 Ladas was a Greek runner, victor in the Olympic games.

4 Rhesus was a Thracian king who fought with the Trojans against the Greeks in Homer's *Iliad.*

59 LOW RENT

These figures are all unknown.

60 CLASSIC INSULT

1 Scylla was a mythological monster in Homer's *Odyssey* who, with the help of her counterpart Charybdis, trapped boats in the strait between Italy and Sicily.

61 WEDDING SONG (EPITHALAMION I)

Poems 61 and 62 are epithalamia, poems composed for and sung to celebrate marriage. Ellipses indicate lines missing from the manuscripts throughout the poem.

1–4 Hymen, the Greek god of marriage, is called the "Child of Helicon's Muse" because the Muses were thought to live on Mount Helicon, and Hymen was considered the son of the Muse Urania, whose name, like Hymen's, we omit. Mount Helicon is located in the region of Greece known as Boeotia overlooking the Gulf of Corinth.

14 Junia and Manlius are the bride and groom. This poem appears to commemorate the marriage of Manlius Torquatus, who may be L. Manlius Torquatus, praetor in 49 BC and member of a well-known Roman family whom Cicero mentions as an Epicurean (Quinn, *Catullus*, 265). Whether this Manlius is the Manlius who appears in the fraught manuscripts of poem 68 (see p. 205) is impossible to say.

16 In the mythological episode known as the Judgment of Paris, Paris, son of the Trojan king Priam, is asked to judge a beauty contest among three goddesses: Aphrodite, Athena, and Hera. The contest occurred after the wedding of Peleus and Thetis (see poem 64) when Eris (the Greek goddess of strife), who had not been invited to the wedding, threw an apple inscribed "for the most beautiful" into the crowd. Paris names Aphrodite most beautiful, in some versions of the myth having been bribed by the promise of Helen. The Judgment of Paris is an important mythological prequel to the Trojan War and Homer's *Iliad*, although the episode is mentioned only briefly near the end of the epic.

18 Lydian refers to a region of what is now western Turkey.

20 We omit the name of the specific nymphs, the Hamadryades.

23–4 In the Latin poem, Mount Helicon is called "the Aonian caves of the rock of Thespiae." Thespiae lay at the base of Mount Helicon.

26 Aganippe was a spring on Mount Helicon, sacred to the Muses.

80   The name Ocean evokes here an early Greek mythological notion of a personified river that surrounds the world. As a god, Oceanus was a Titan and the husband of Tethys.

109–10   We omit the name of this traditional genre, the *versus Fescennini*.

114–15   *puer delicatus* is the Latin term for a favorite slave boy used as a sexual toy by his master.

117   The marriage god named here is not Hymen but the Roman Talassio.

182   Baby Torquatus is imagined as the product of the union of Junia and Manlius.

192   Penelope was the wife of Odysseus, famous for her fidelity during his absence of approximately twenty years chronicled in Homer's *Iliad* and *Odyssey*.

192   Telemachus was the son of Odysseus and Penelope.

62 BRIDAL AGON (EPITHALAMION II)

3   Vesper is the evening star, sometimes personified, the Roman equivalent of Hesperus.

10   Here we omit two epithets of Vesper (Evening): Oetaeos (from the name of a mountain between Thessaly and Aetolia) and Noctifer (Night-Bearing).

40–1   Lines are missing from the manuscripts, as indicated by our ellipses.

63 WILD SIDE

Title A nod to Lou Reed. Catullus' use of the feminine pronoun following Attis' castration and the subsequent ambiguity of Attis' gender in the Latin is fascinating and has caused much consternation among those studying the manuscripts, not to mention those translating.

2   All that can be said unequivocally about Attis is that in the narrative of the poem, Attis is a Greek follower of Cybele.

10   Cybele was a Phrygian goddess known also as the Magna Mater (Great Mother) or the Mistress of Dindymus. Hers was a religion of initiation, a mystery cult, introduced to Italy during the Roman Republic.

13   Gallae is the feminine Latin form of the name for followers of Cybele, who were castrated men.

14 Dindymene is another name for Cybele taken from the name Dindymus, the Phrygian mountain home of the goddess. In the Latin, the genitive *Dindymenae* properly modifies *dominae*, the goddess; here we craft an intentionally ambiguous line in which the Dindymenae may be the feminine plural followers of Cybele, like Gallae, or a possessive genitive following flock, as in "the flock belonging to the goddess from Dindymus."

29 Maenads are followers of Dionysus or Bacchus, whose rites are similar to those of Cybele.

43 Hypnos was the Greek god of sleep and brother of Thanatos (Death).

50 In Greek mythology, Pasithea is one of the three Graces (Charites) and the wife of Hypnos.

60 Mount Ida, like Mount Dindymus, is in Phrygia.

64 EPYLLION

Title Epyllion is the diminutive of epic. See Quinn (*Catullus*, 298–9) for a clear outline of the Latin poem's complex structure. We employ line breaks and quotation marks to lend clarity to the narrative.

2 Mount Pelion, mythological home of Chiron, the centaur fabled to have tutored Achilles, is located in Thessaly in central Greece. The mountain is named for Achilles' father Peleus, whose marriage to Thetis provides the narrative frame of poem 64.

3 Poseidon is the Greek god of the sea, earthquakes, and horses; in contrast with Athena, whose domain, broadly speaking, is human technology, Poseidon is a god of natural power, a force of nature; he is often called "Earth-Shaker."

4 The Phasis River is located in what is now western Georgia and is known as the Rion or Rioni River. This region of Georgia was known to the Greeks as Colchis, home of Medea, Jason's erstwhile savior and beloved. In his *Argonautica*, Apollonius of Rhodes writes about Jason sailing the Phasis River in the Argo in order to reach Colchis and obtain the Golden Fleece. This nod to the story of Jason, who eventually abandons Medea, anticipates the analogous story of Theseus, who abandons Ariadne on Naxos en route to Greece. We omit here the name of Medea's father, Aeëtes: Catullus calls Colchis "the lands of Aeëtes."

7 This line is intended to call to mind the Greek term *kleos*, the coveted goal of all Homeric heroes whose best translation is "immortal fame." *Kleos* is

the fame of a hero that in some way mitigates the fact of his death by allowing his name to survive eternally.

12 This is Athena, Greek goddess of war, wisdom, and weaving and patron goddess of the city of Athens. Athena's tripartite realm comprises three fields of human technology and strategy, and here Athena is credited with having built Jason's ship, the Argo.

15 Corruption in the manuscripts prevents us from determining whether the Argo is being characterized as the first ship ever to sail the sea or whether the implication is that Athena launched the Argo herself. Thus, in our translation, the meaning of "first" is intentionally left ambiguous.

16 Amphitrite is the divine wife of Neptune/Poseidon, used here as metonymy for the sea.

20 Nereids are divine sea nymphs.

26 Peleus was a Greek hero, one of the Argonauts who sailed with Jason, and the mortal who fell in love with the Nereid Thetis. The wedding of Peleus and Thetis not only provides the narrative frame for poem 64 but is also the occasion immediately preceding the mythological episode known as the Judgment of Paris, an ostensible cause of the Trojan War, in which Peleus and Thetis' son Achilles would die and gain great fame (*kleos*).

36 Rather than name Thetis' mother Doris, Catullus shows his erudition by naming her grandparents, Tethys and Ocean.

43 Cieros and the city names that follow are all located in Thessaly. Cieros is attested by Strabo but is otherwise obscure (Quinn, *Catullus*, 307).

44 Tempe is in northern Thessaly, strangely far from Phthia, a city in southern Thessaly that gives us the Latin adjective *Phthiotica*. Phthia was the birthplace of Achilles, however, so the mythological reference may have outweighed the geographical in this case. Crannon and Larissa are both in central Thessaly.

45 Pharsalia was the region of Thessaly in which the city of Pharsalus was located: some translators print Pharsalus here, depending on the Latin edition that they follow.

63 Catullus now moves from the poem's introductory frame to its ekphrasis, the description of the scene woven into the coverlet. Ariadne was the daughter of King Minos of Crete who helped Theseus slay her half-brother, the Minotaur, the offspring of Pasiphae and the Cretan Bull. The Minotaur so terrorized the island that he was enclosed in the famous labyrinth.

65 Catullus calls the island Dia, not Naxos. A small island called Dia does · exist near Crete, but by the Hellenistic period, there was general agreement that the site of Ariadne's abandonment by Theseus was Naxos; as Catullus so often does, we follow Hellenistic tradition here.

66 Theseus was the Athenian hero who traveled to Crete to slay the Minotaur and free the Athenians from the bloody annual tribute required as recompense for their murder of Minos' son Androgeos. Catullus implies that the pollution from the murder caused a plague at Athens requiring the sacrifice of young men and women to the Minotaur.

74 Minoan refers to the island of Crete and comes from the name of the Bronze Age civilization on the island.

86 Piraeus is the port of Athens.

87 Catullus calls our "island palace" the *Gortynia templa*. We omit the specific reference to Gortyn, a city in Crete famous for the Gortyn Code, the oldest extant example of a Greek law code.

88 The harsh-judging king is King Minos of Crete.

89 Here Catullus calls Aphrodite *Erycina*, "Lady of Eryx," referring to Eryx in Sicily (now Erice), home of an ancient cult site of Aphrodite/Venus. We omit the reference.

95 We omit here and elsewhere references to Athens as the city of Cecrops. Cecrops was a mythical founder and hero of the city of Athens.

108 The Eurotas River is one of the main rivers of the Greek Peloponnese.

113 Eros is the son of Aphrodite, a Greek god of love and desire in his own right and counterpart of the Roman Cupid.

130 Taurian here means from the Taurus Mountains in what is now southern Turkey, not to be confused with our "taurine" in line 252, referring to a bull.

154 Our use of the word "complaint" in this line is pointed. What follows is a classic example of what has been called *querela*, a genre of complaint perhaps best exemplified in Latin literature by Ovid's *Heroides*, in which Ariadne again has her say to Theseus, as does Medea to Jason and likewise do many other female figures similarly wronged by lovers.

178 Syrtes refers to two bodies of water near North Africa known to be extremely dangerous to sailors because of their shallows rife with quicksand.

212 The Furies, also called the Erinyes or the Eumenides, were archaic goddesses of vengeance who ensured the payment of blood prices.

223 The celestial judge is Jupiter/Zeus.

233 Aegeus is Theseus' father.

250 Iton refers to a famous sanctuary of Athena in Thessaly.

251 Erectheus was an archaic king of Athens who was considered the earthly incarnation of Poseidon; an earlier reference to Erectheus in line 211 of the Latin was omitted in translation.

271 Sileni are satyr-like worshippers of Bacchus/Dionysus. Here they are called *Nysigenis*, born at Nysa, one of the mythological birthplaces of Bacchus/Dionysus and/or his cult.

274 *Euhoe!* is the traditional cry of the worshippers of Bacchus/Dionysus.

288 Zephyr is called by his Latin name Favonius in this poem.

304 Penios is the personification of the Thessalian river of the same name.

306 Phaethon is the mythological son of the Sun (either Apollo or Helios) who was killed in a hubristic attempt to drive his father's chariot across the sky. His grieving sisters were changed into poplars.

310 Prometheus is a Titan, a trickster figure in Greek mythology and champion of human beings who stole fire from the gods in order to enhance human culture. In some stories, Prometheus is even credited with the creation of human beings. For flouting Zeus' authority, Prometheus was chained to the face of a cliff where each day an eagle pecked out his liver and each night it grew back in order for his torture to continue the following day.

314 Phoebus is Phoebus Apollo, Greek and Roman god of music and the sun, poetry and prophecy, and twin brother of Artemis, whose Roman equivalent is Diana.

315 We omit a reference to Idrus, probably a reference to an unknown mythical founder of Idrias, a town in Caria known for the worship of Hecate, Greek counterpart of Trivia/Diana. As Quinn notes, the reading is "suspect" (*Catullus*, 338), and little is lost in the omission.

319 The Fates, known in Greek as *Moirai* and in Latin as *Parcae*, are elderly goddesses thought to spin (and eventually cut) the thread of life for each human being.

335 Emathia is a name used for the personification of two geographical regions, Macedonia and Thessaly. Jove is called in the Latin "the son of Ops," Roman goddess of wealth and abundance who was married to Saturn.

357 Teucrian refers to the people of Troy, whose earliest mythological king was Teucer.

358 Pelops was the son of Tantalus and father of Atreus, whose doomed
house is chronicled in Aeschylus' *Oresteia*. The Peloponnese is named for
Pelops, and he had a cult at Olympia as one of the founders of the
Olympic games.

359 Troy, the site of the Trojan War, is located in what is now northwestern
Turkey.

370 The Scamander is the river made angry in Homer's *Iliad* when Achilles
chokes it with dead bodies.

371 The Hellespont, known now as the Dardanelles, is a narrow strait
dividing Europe from Turkey and connecting the Aegean with the Sea
of Marmara.

382 In post-Homeric mythology, Polyxena, youngest daughter of the Trojan
king and queen Priam and Hecuba, appears to have developed some sort
of relationship with Achilles after the death of Patroclus. In Euripides'
Trojan Women and *Hecuba*, Polyxena is sacrificed on the grave of Achilles
so that the Greeks might return home safely, mirroring the sacrifice of
Iphigeneia by Agamemnon that preceded the Greeks' setting forth from
Aulis in order to attack Troy.

405 Mount Parnassus looms over the Sanctuary of Apollo at Delphi.

406 Delphi was a sanctuary site of Apollo near Mount Parnassus, the
so-called omphalos (navel or belly button) of the world, and the home
of the Pythia and the Delphic oracle, the most powerful and well-known
oracle in the ancient world.

408 Mars is the Roman god of war, the Roman equivalent of Ares.

65 LIKE AN APPLE

This poem introduces the translation that follows (poem 66). Irregularities in
the meter suggest that line 9 of the Latin poem is missing.

1 Hortalus is probably the Hortensius of poem 95ab and may be the orator
and poet Q. Hortensius Hortalus, (Quinn, *Catullus*, 351).

5 Lethe is the stream in the Underworld that induces forgetting, relieving
the dead of their memories of life and thereby their suffering and, in some
schools of thought, preparing them for their next life.

8 Rhoetean refers to a promontory near Troy but is often taken synony-
mously for Troy itself.

12 Procne, called Daulias in the Latin because of her husband's roots (Tereus
lived in Daulis in Phocis), killed her son Itys to take revenge on Tereus for

raping her sister, Philomela. In her myth, Procne eventually turned into a nightingale.

13 Itys (also called Itylus) was the son Procne killed.

15 Because we use it in the title of poem 66, we omit from this poem the identification of the translated poem as *haec carmina Battiadae*, "this poem of Callimachus."

66 CALLIMACHUS' LOCK OF BERENICE

Like poem 51, poem 66 is Catullus' translation of a Greek poem, this time from the fourth book of Callimachus' *Aetia*. Of Callimachus' original, only fragments remain.

6 Endymion was the mortal lover of Trivia (or Selene) the moon goddess. We omit here the name Trivia and a reference to the location of their tryst, Mount Latmus in Caria, a region of what is now Turkey.

7 Conon was an astronomer in the court of Ptolemy III in Egypt.

8 Queen Berenice was the wife of Ptolemy III of Egypt.

43 In Greek mythology, Helios is the sun; Catullus here calls him the "son of Thia."

42–7 Xerxes of Persia dug a canal through the isthmus that connected Mount Athos to Macedonia, the implication being that not even a mountain like Athos could resist being severed once humans had the power of steel.

48 Catullus names these first miners, the Chalybes, but we omit the name.

51–2 These lines, typical of a poet like Callimachus, include witty mythological play and allusion to the west wind Zephyrus, his twin brother Memnon of Ethiopia, and Arsinoë, the late wife of Ptolemy II who upon death was associated with Aphrodite Zephiritis, so named for the Aphrodite temple in the city of Zephyrium. Zephyrus, here conflated with Pegasus, combined with a play on the name of the city, together imply that the dead queen had the power to command the west wind to deliver Berenice's hair to the heavens. Arsinoë is also called *Locridos*, but it is unclear why or to which Locris Catullus refers. See Quinn, *Catullus*, 362–3.

56 Canopic is a reference to the Egyptian city of Canopus near Alexandria and its well-known serapeum (temple of Serapis).

64 Virgo and Leo are constellations.

64 Lycaon was a king of Arcadia and the father of Callisto, who was turned into a bear and then a constellation (Ursa Major).

65 Callisto and Boötes are constellations.

67 Tethys was a Titan, sister and wife of Ocean, goddess of the sea.

89 Orion is a constellation.

90 Aquarius is a constellation.

67 DIALOGUE AT VERONA

5 The name Balbus appears only here, and Balbus is otherwise unknown.

12 A Caecilius appears in poem 35, but this may be another man of the same name.

41 Brixia is the modern city of Brescia in northern Italy west of Verona.

41 The Mella is a river in northern Italy known by the same name today.

43 Cycnus was a mythological figure famous for having turned into a swan after mourning his beloved Phaethon; he was a native of Liguria, a region of Italy on the northwestern coast whose capital is Genoa.

46 Postumius and Cornelius cannot be identified with certainty. A Cornelius appears in poems 1 and 102, but we cannot know whether this Cornelius corresponds to either.

68 ODE TO A FRIEND

This poem is one of the most difficult in the corpus because its manuscripts preserve not only multiple addressees but also both second and third person narration. In some translations poem 68 is taken as two poems, 68a and 68b. Martin presents it as one poem, Green as two, with 68a ending after our line 41 where the name in the manuscripts changes from Mallius (in some versions Manlius) to Allius and where the introductory epistle seems to become the promised poem. Our understanding and interpretation of the poem argues for unity, which we attempt to provide: Catullus sends a note promising a poem and follows with the poem itself. Rather than choose among the three addressees, whose names, in any case, seem more likely to be corruptions of one name than three distinct people in two different poems, we do not name an addressee at all but simply address the poem to a friend. For specifics on the fascinating structure and manuscript tradition of the poem, see Quinn, *Catullus*, 373–96.

55 Thermopylae means "Hot Gates" in Greek, so named for the hot springs and fabled entrances to Hades nearby. This pass near the Gulf of Malia was the only route between Lokris and Thessaly that could, in ancient times, accommodate an army of any size, and it was therefore the site of many battles, most famously the battle between a relatively small Greek force (including the 300 Spartans chronicled in the films *The 300 Spartans*, 1962, and *300*, 2006) and the army of Xerxes in 480 BC.

71 In Greek and Roman mythology, Laodamia, wife of Protesilaus, was inconsolable after her husband's death at Troy and eventually committed suicide. Catullus' characterization of the couple as having shirked their sacrificial duty is unattested elsewhere.

73 Protesilaus, husband of Laodamia, was a warrior from Thessaly who fought and was killed at Troy.

85 In Greek and Roman mythology, the Trojan War ostensibly began when Helen (either by her own will or by force, depending on which version you read) ended up with Paris in Troy rather than with her husband, Menelaus, in Sparta. Of course, as Homer makes clear in the *Iliad*, there were many reasons people went to war at Troy, only one of which was to avenge the loss of Helen.

106 Arcadian Cyllene is a mountain in southern Greece (Arcadia) personified as a nymph in Greek and Roman mythology. Catullus names in the Latin the specific city with the "rich ground," Pheneus: we omit the name.

109 For his sixth labor, Heracles was asked to drive away a huge flock of birds from Stymphalos, modern Stymfalia. In the Latin, Catullus calls Heracles by the pseudo-patronymic Amphitryoniades; in truth, Amphitryon was Heracles' stepfather: Heracles was the son of Zeus.

112 Hebe is a daughter of Zeus and Hera, goddess of youth in her own right and the wife of Heracles upon his assumption to Mount Olympus.

133 Hera is the wife of Zeus in Greek mythology, a queenly goddess and also goddess of marriage; her Roman equivalent is Juno.

147 Themis is the Greek goddess of law and order, a Titan.

69 NO BEAUTIES FOR THE BEAST

1 The name Rufus appears in poem 77 as well. Identifications of Rufus are speculative; however, Green is not alone in claiming that Rufus is M. Caelius Rufus, perhaps also the Caelius of poems 58 and 100 (Peter Green, *The Poems of Catullus: A Bilingual Edition* (University of California

Press, 2005): 279), although the Caelius of 100 appears to hail from Verona, whereas M. Caelius Rufus was from modern Teramo.

72 ONCE

This poem capitalizes on a beautiful ambiguity in Latin that makes it impossible in certain instances to distinguish the subject from the direct object in reported speech (*oratio obliqua*), hence our parenthetical.

74 UNCLE HARPOCRATES

Title Harpocrates was an Egyptian god depicted with his finger at his lips.

1 Gellius is generally agreed to be L. Gellius Poplicola, a "radical young man" (Green, *Poems*, 290) in Catullus' social circle; the name also appears in poems 80, 88, 89, 90, 91, and 116.

75 EXHAUSTION

2 *tua culpa* is Latin for "your fault" as *mea culpa* is for "my fault."

78 ALL IN THE FAMILY I

1 Gallus is an unknown figure.

79 HER BROTHER

1 Scholars generally agree that Lesbius is Lesbia's brother, and while this cannot be proven, it is a natural assumption based on Roman naming conventions, as seen with Clodius and Clodia on 17–18.

82 ALL EYES

1 Quintius, also named in poem 100, is an unknown figure, but he may be the brother of the Quintia of poem 86, based again on Roman naming conventions.

84 PUTTING ON HAIRS

1 It is tempting to identify Arrius as the orator Q. Arrius, as does Skinner.[3] Q. Arrius was a supporter of Crassus who served in Syria and was panned by Cicero (*Brut.* 242–43). See Green, *Poems* 275.

85 ODETAMO

Title The title of this poem is the first three words of the Latin poem (*odi et amo*) elided, as they would have sounded, making the verbal ideas of loving and hating come together as if in a single verb. See p. 18.

95AB CINNA'S EPIC REDUCTION

Some read the last two lines of our translation as a separate fragment, calling it 95b, but Martin and Green also treat it as one poem. Line 4 is missing from the Latin.

2 Cinna, probably also the Cinna of poems 10 and 113, usually thought synonymous with Gaius Helvius Cinna, was the author of an epyllion like Catullus' poem 64; three lines of this work survive. See W. Morel's *Fragmenta Poetarum Latinorum* (Teubner, 1963), 88; E. Courtney's *The Fragmentary Latin Poets* (Oxford University Press, 2003), 212–224; and A. S. Hollis', *Fragments of Roman Poetry* (Oxford University Press, 2009), 11–48.

2 "Zmyrna" is the name of Cinna's epyllion, whose topic was the incestuous love of Zmyrna (also known as Smyrna and Myrrha) for her father Cinyras.

3 Hortensius is probably the Q. Hortensius Hortalus of poem 65.

6 The "river it celebrates" is the Satrachus in Cyprus, whose name we omit.

7 Volusius wrote the "shitty scraps" of poem 36.

11 Antimachus of Colophon, fifth–fourth century BC Greek author of the "Lyde" and a "Thebaid," was panned by Callimachus for his lack of concision.

96 LEGACY

1 Later evidence from Propertius and Ovid on the lost works of Calvus has led to general agreement that this Quintilia was the wife of M. Licinius

[3] Marilyn Skinner, *Catullus in Verona: A Reading of the Elegaic Libellus, Poems 65–116* (Columbus, Ohio, , 2003): 104–107.

Macer Calvus of poems 14, 50, and 53 (perhaps called Licinius in 50). See Quinn, *Catullus*, 433–4. Here we omit Calvus' name.

97   ALL KINDS OF ASS

1 Aemilius appears only here and cannot be clearly identified with any single historical figure, although there are a number of likely candidates.

98   BAD BREATH

1 The name Victus appears only here and cannot be identified with an historical figure.

100   BROTHERLY LOVE (AUFILLENA I)

1 This may be M. Caelius Rufus, but it may not: it may be the Caelius of poem 58. Quintius is unknown historically but may be the Quintius of poem 82, perhaps the brother of the Quintia in poem 86.
2 The siblings Aufillenus and Aufillena are unknown.

101   AVE ATQUE VALE

Title *Ave atque vale* are the final three words of the Latin poem, oft quoted untranslated by classicists: "be well and farewell."

102   SHHH …

4 It is impossible to say whether this is the Cornelius Nepos of poem 1, the unknown Cornelius of 67, or another Cornelius altogether.

103   A PROPER PIMP

1 We omit the name of the unknown pimp, Silo.

104   THE LAST WORD ON LESBIA

Title Our title is speculative.

4 We omit the name of the addressee's unknown accomplice, Tappo.

105 THE ADVENTURES OF LITTLE PRICK II

1 We omit the name Pipla, which refers to a spring sacred to the Muses on Mount Olympus.

108 COMINIUS: DOTAGE DISMEMBERED

Title Cominius, the addressee of the Latin poem, appears only here and is otherwise unknown; we relegate his name to the title.

111 ALL IN THE FAMILY IV (AUFILLENA III)

Syllables are missing from the final line of the Latin poem.

112 UNKNOWN NASO

1 Naso is unknown: our title says it all.

113 BY THE NUMBERS

1 This may be the Cinna of poems 10 and 95ab.
2 Maecilia is unknown; Green instead gives Mucillam, diminutive of Mucia, and identifies her as the daughter of Q. Mucius Scaevola (Green *Poems*, 299). The name Maecilia is well enough attested, however, that the emendation is not necessary. Since fifteen years elapsed between Pompey's two consulships, the implication is that the years have taken a toll on Maecilia.

114 THE ADVENTURES OF LITTLE PRICK III

1 The first word of the Latin poem locates the estate at Firmum, modern Fermo; we omit the specific reference.

115 THE ADVENTURES OF LITTLE PRICK IV

3 Croesus was a king of Lydia in the sixth century BC. He was famous for his wealth and is well known from a story reported by Herodotus in which he questions Solon as to which man was born most blessed and is surprised to find that Solon does not name him.

6–7 The "Northern Lights" refers here to the Hyperboreans, mythical inhabitants of a mythical northern land.

116 ARCHERY

3 The "poems of sacred Battus" are the poems of Callimachus.
6 This is probably the Gellius of poems 74 et al.

Works cited

Barnard, Mary and Fitts, Dudley. *Sappho: A New Translation*. University of California Press, 1958.

Benjamin, Walter, "The Task of the Translator." In *Illuminations*, trans. Harry Zohn. Random House, 2007: 63–82.

Bickel, E. "Catulli in Caesarem carmina," *Rheinisches Museum* 93 (1949: 13–20).

Bradley, Adam and Dubois, Andrew, eds. *The Anthology of Rap*. Yale University Press, 2010.

Copjec, Joan. *Read My Desire*. MIT Press, 1994.

Courtney, Edward. *The Fragmentary Latin Poets*, revised edition. Oxford University Press, 2003.

Dillon, Matthew and Garland, Lynda. *Ancient Rome: From the Early Republic to the Assassination of Julius Caesar*. Routledge, 2005.

Foucault, Michel. *The History of Sexuality*, vol. 2: *The Use of Pleasure*. Vintage, 1990.

Gratwick, A. S. "*Vale, Patrona Virgo*: The Text of Catullus 1.9," *Classical Quarterly* 52.1 (2002): 305–320.

Green, Peter. *The Poems of Catullus: A Bilingual Edition*. University of California Press, 2005.

Hejduk, Julia Dyson. *Clodia: A Sourcebook*. University of Oklahoma Press, 2008.

Hollis, Adrian S. *Fragments of Roman Poetry ca. 60 BC–AD 20*. Oxford University Press, 2009.

Homer. *Odyssey*. Trans. Robert Fagles. Penguin Classics, 1999.
  Odyssey. Trans. Stanley Lombardo. Hackett Publishing Company, 2000.

Janan, Micaela. *"When the Lamp is Shattered": Desire and Narrative in Catullus*. Southern Illinois University Press, 1994.

Loomis, Julia W. "M. Furius Bibaculus and Catullus," *Classical World* 63.4 (1969): 112–114.

Martin, Charles. *The Poems of Catullus*. The Johns Hopkins University Press, 1989.

Miller, Paul Allen. *Lyric Texts and Lyric Consciousness*. Routledge, 1994.

Mitchell, Juliet and Rose, Jacqueline, eds. *Feminine Sexuality: Jacques Lacan and the école freudienne*. W. W. Norton and Company, 1985.

Works cited

Morel, W., ed. *Fragmenta Poetarum Latinorum*. Teubner, 1963 (reprint).

Neudling, Chester L. *A Prosopography to Catullus*. Iowa Studies in Classical Philology 12. Oxford, 1955.

Plato. *Symposium*. Trans. Alexander Nehamas and Paul Woodruff. Hackett Publishing Company, 1989.

Quinn, Kenneth. *Catullus: The Poems*. St. Martin's Press, 1973.

Rayor, Diane. *Sappho: A New Translation of the Complete Works*. Cambridge University Press, 2014.

Reynolds, L. D. and Wilson, N. G. *Scribes and Scholars*. Oxford University Press, 1991.

Richlin, Amy. *Rome and the Mysterious Orient: Three Plays by Plautus*. University of California Press, 2005.

Skinner, Marilyn. *Clodia Metelli: The Tribune's Sister*. Oxford University Press, 2011.
    Catullus in Verona: A Reading of the Elegaic Libellus, Poems 65–116. Columbus, Ohio, 2003.
    Catullus' Passer. Ayer, 1992.

Syme, Ronald. *The Roman Revolution*, revised edition. Oxford University Press, 2002.

Wills, Garry. *Martial's Epigrams: A Selection*. Viking Adult, 2008.

Wiseman, T. P. *Roman Political Life*. University of Exeter Press, 1985.

Glossary of Proper Names

Acme (45.1): unknown

Adonis (29.9): mythological figure famous for his beauty, object of **Aphrodite's** and Persephone's affections

Aegeus (64.233): father of **Theseus**

Aemilius (97.1): unknown

Aganippe (61.26): a spring on Mt. **Helicon** sacred to the **Muses**

Alfenus (30.1): unknown, perhaps the lawyer Alfenus Varus and the **Varus** of poems 10 and 22

Amathos (36.13): a city in Cyprus

Ameana (41.1): unknown, perhaps the girlfriend of **Mamurra**

Amphitrite (64.16): Greek goddess of the sea and wife of **Poseidon**

Ancon/Ancona (36.13): a city on the Adriatic Sea northeast of Rome

Androgeos (64.94): son of King **Minos** of Crete

Antimachus of Colophon (95ab.11): fifth-fourth-century BC Greek author

Antius (44.9): unknown, perhaps C. Antius Restio

Aphrodite (36.1, 64): Greek goddess of love and desire, counterpart of the Roman **Venus**

Aquarius (66.90): the constellation

Aquinus (14.16): unknown

Arcadian (68.106): adjective referring to Arcadia in southern Greece

Ariadne (64.63): daughter of King Minos of Crete who helped **Theseus** slay her half-brother the Minotaur

Arrius (84.1): probably the orator Q. Arrius

Arsinoë (66.52): the late wife of Ptolemy II of Egypt

Asinius (12.1): Asinius Marrucinus

Atalanta (2ab) mythological huntress who wished to remain a virgin forever

Athena (64.12): Greek goddess of war, wisdom, and weaving, counterpart of the Roman Minerva

Attis (63.2): unknown

Aufillena (100.2): unknown, probably the sister of **Aufillenus**

Aufillenus (100.2): unknown, probably the brother of **Aufillena**

Aurelius (11.1, 15, 16, 21): unknown

Aurora (11.3): Roman goddess of the dawn

Bacchus (27.7): Roman god of wine, counterpart of the Greek Dionysus

Balbus (67.5): unknown

Battus (7.6, 116): first king of the Greek colony whose capital was **Cyrene**, thereby making indirect reference to the poet Callimachus

Berenice (66.8): wife of Ptolemy III of Egypt

Bithynia (10.6): a Roman province in what is now northwest Turkey

Boötes (66.65): the constellation

Brits (11.9): an adjective referring to the peoples of Roman Britain

Brixia (67.41): modern Brescia

Caecilius (35.1, 67): unknown

Caelius: (58.1, 100): perhaps M. Caelius Rufus; see **Rufus**

Caesar (11.7): Gaius Julius Caesar

Caesius (14.16): unknown

Callisto (66.65): the constellation

Calvus: (14.1, 50, 53): probably C. Licinius Macer Calvus, who is probably also the **Licinius** of poem 50

Camerius (55.8, 58b): unknown

Campus Minor (55.3): otherwise unattested

Canopic (66.56): adjective referring to the Egyptian city of Canopus

Castor and Pollux (4.23, 68): divine twin brothers, children of Leda

Cato (56.1): probably the poet P. Valerius Cato

Cicero (49.1): Marcus Tullius Cicero, famous orator, politician, and philosopher

Cieros (64.43): a city in **Thessaly**

Cinna (10.26, 95ab, 113): probably the poet Gaius Helvius Cinna

Circus Maximus (55.3–4): an ancient Roman stadium

Cominius (108): unknown

Conon (66.7): astronomer in the court of Ptolemy III in Egypt

Cornelius (1.3, 67, 102): in poem 1, probably Cornelius Nepos

Cornificius (38.1): perhaps Quintus Cornificius, orator and poet

Crannon (64.44): a city in central **Thessaly**

Croesus (115.3): sixth-century BC king of **Lydia**

Cupid (3.1, 36, 68): **Venus'** son and a god of love and desire in his own right, Roman counterpart of the Greek **Eros**

Cybele (35.11, 63): the **Phrygian** Great Mother Goddess

Cycnus (67.43): a mythological figure who turned into a swan

Cyllene (68.106): a mountain in Arcadia personified as a nymph in Greek and Roman mythology

Cyrene (7.3): a city in northern Libya, birthplace of the poet Callimachus

Cytorian (4.11): adjective referring to the city of Cytorus on the Black Sea

Delphi (64.406): sanctuary site of **Apollo** near **Mt. Parnassus**

Diana (34.1): Roman goddess of the moon, the hunt, and childbirth, counterpart of the Greek Artemis and, like Artemis, a perpetual virgin

Dindymenae (63.14): followers of **Cybele**

Dindymene (63.14): see **Cybele**

Dyrrachion (36.14): a port city on the coast of Illyria opposite what is now Brindisi

Egnatius (37.1, 39): unknown

Emathia (64.335): Macedonia and **Thessaly**

Endymion (66.6): mortal lover of **Trivia** (or Selene) the moon goddess

Erectheus (64.251): archaic king of Athens, considered the earthly incarnation of **Poseidon**

Eros (64.113): son of **Aphrodite** and Greek god of love and desire, counterpart of the Roman **Cupid**

Etruscan (39.12): adjective referring to an ancient region of Italy encompassing Tuscany, western Umbria, and northern Latium (Lazio) and the culture thereof

Eurotas (64.108): one of the main rivers of the Greek Peloponnese

Fabullus (12.17, 13, 28, 47): unknown

Fates (64.319, 68): goddesses thought to spin the thread of life for each human being

Falernian (27.1): one of the most famous and well-regarded wines produced in Catullus' time

Flavius (6.1): unknown

Fufidius (54.6): unknown

Furies (64.212): also called the Erinyes or Eumenides, archaic goddesses of vengeance who ensured the payment of blood prices

Furius (11.1, 16, 23, 26): perhaps the poet M. Furius Bibaculus

Gaius (10.26): see **Cinna**

Gallae (63.13): eunuch followers of the goddess **Cybele**

Gallic (11.8): adjective referring to a region comprising what is now primarily France

Gallus (78.1): unknown

Gellius: (74.1, 80, 88, 89, 90, 91, 116): probably L. Gellius Poplicola

Golgi (36.13): a city in Cyprus

Harpocrates (74): Egyptian god of silence

Hebe (68.112): Greek goddess of youth

Helen (68.85): daughter of **Zeus** and Leda, known both as Helen of Sparta and Helen of **Troy**

Helicon (61.1–4): Mt. Helicon, home of the **Muses**

Helios (66.43): Greek name for the sun and the sun god

Hellespont (64.371): the modern Dardanelles

Hera (68.133): Greek queen of the gods, wife of **Zeus**, and goddess of marriage, counterpart of the Roman **Juno**

Heracles (55.12): a Greek mythological figure famous for his twelve labors

Hirrus (54.3): unknown

Hortalus (65.1), perhaps the orator and poet Q. **Hortensius** Hortalus

Hortensius (95ab.3): perhaps Q. Hortensius **Hortalus**

Hot Gates (68.55): Thermopylae in Greek

Hymen (61.22): Greek god of marriage

Hypnos (63.43): Greek god of sleep

Idalion (36.11): an ancient city in Cyprus

Ipsitilla (32.1): unknown

Iton (64.250): sanctuary of Athena in **Thessaly**

Itys (65.13): a mythological figure killed by his mother **Procne** to avenge her husband's rape of her sister

Jove (7.5): another name for **Jupiter**

Junia (61.14): bride of **Manlius**

Juno Lucina (34.13): Roman goddess of childbirth

Jupiter (4.19) the Roman sky god, father and political head of the Roman pantheon and counterpart of the Greek **Zeus**, also called **Jove**

Juventius: (24.2, 48, 81, 99): while Juventius himself is unknown, a family of Juventii is attested at Rome at this time

Knidos (36.13): an ancient Greek city in Caria, modern southwestern Turkey

Ladas (58b.3): a Greek runner, victor in the Olympic games

Lanuvian (39.13): adjective referring to the ancient city Lanuvium in Latium (modern Lanuvio)

Laodamia (68.71): wife of **Protesilaus**

Larissa (64.45): a city in central **Thessaly**

Latona (34.5): mother of the goddess **Diana**

Leo (66.64): the constellation

Lesbia: (5.17, 43, 51, 58, 70, 72, 75, 83, 86, 87, 92, 104, 107): the name given to Catullus' primary female love interest

Lesbius (79.1): perhaps **Lesbia's** brother

Lethe (65.4): a stream in the Underworld that induces forgetting

Libo (54.4): perhaps L. Scribonius Libo

Licinius (50.1): probably C. Licinius Macer Calvus; see **Calvus**

Ligurian (17.20): an adjective referring to a northwestern coastal region of Italy

Lycaon (66.64): king of Arcadia and the father of **Callisto**

Lydian (61.18): adjective referring to a region in what is now western Turkey

Maecilia (113.2): unknown

Maenads (63.29, 64): female followers of **Bacchus**/Dionysus

Mamurra (29.3, 57): historical figure who served in the foreign campaigns of **Caesar** and **Pompey**

Manlius (61.14): perhaps L. Manlius **Torquatus**

Marmara (4.7): a region on the Black Sea in what is now northwestern Turkey

Mars (64.408): Roman god of war, counterpart of the Greek Ares

Mella (67.41): a river in northern Italy

Memmius (28.7): governor of **Bithynia**

Memnon (66.51): king of Ethiopia, twin brother of **Zephyr(us)**

Menenius (59.1): unknown

Midas (24.4): a mythical king of **Phrygia** who wished that everything he touched might turn to gold

Minoan (64.74): the Bronze Age civilization on Crete

Minos (64.103): king of Crete, "harsh-judging king" of 64.88, and father of **Ariadne** and **Androgeos**

Mt. Aetna (68.54): a volcanic mountain on the island of Sicily and the mythological home of Vulcan, Roman god of fire and the forge, counterpart of the Greek Hephaestus

Mt. Athos (66.46): a mountain on the Chalkidiki peninsula in Greece

Mt. Helicon (61.1): mythological home of the **Muses**

Mt. Ida (63.60): a mountain in **Phrygia**

Mt. Parnassus (64.405): the mountain above the Sanctuary of **Apollo** at **Delphi**

Mt. Pelion (64.2): located in **Thessaly** in central Greece

Muse(s): (1.8, 65.4, 68.8 and ff., 105.2) the nine patron goddesses of poetry, literature, history, music, and astronomy

Naso (112.1): unknown

Naxos (64.65): a Cycladic island in the Aegean Sea

Nemesis (50.14, 64, 68): Greek goddess of revenge and retribution

Neptune (31.3): Roman god of the sea, counterpart of the Greek **Poseidon**

Nereids (64.20): sea nymphs of the Mediterranean

Nicaea (46.5): a city in the Roman province **Bithynia**

Nonius (52.2): unknown

Northern Lights (115.6–7): the Hyperboreans, inhabitants of a mythical northern land

Ocean/Oceanus (61.80): a Titan and husband of the goddess **Tethys**

Orcus (3.14): Roman god of the Underworld

Orion (66.89): the constellation

Otho (54.1): unknown

Paris (61.16): son of Priam, husband of **Helen** in Homer's *Iliad*

Pasithea (63.50): one of the Graces, wife of **Hypnos**

Parthian (11.5): adjective referring to a region in what is now northeastern Iran

Pegasus (58b.2): a mythological winged horse, offspring of **Poseidon**

Peleus (64.26): wife of the **Nereid** Thetis and father of Achilles

Pelops (64.358): son of Tantalus and father of Atreus

Penelope (61.192): wife of the Greek hero Odysseus

Penios (64.304): a river in **Thessaly**

Persian (11.4, 66): adjective referring to the inhabitants of the Persian Empire

Phaethon (64.306): the mythological son of the Apollo/**Helios** who perished driving the chariot of the Sun

Pharsalia/Pharsalus (64.45): respectively, a region and city in **Thessaly**

Phasis (64.4): a river located in what is now western Georgia, known now as the Rion or Rioni

Phoebus (64.314): Phoebus Apollo, Greek and Roman god of music and the sun, poetry and prophecy

Phrygia/Phrygian (46.1, 63.22, 64): a region in what is now central Turkey, home of the goddess **Cybele**

Phthia (64.44): a city in southern **Thessaly**, birthplace of Achilles

Piraeus (64.86): the port of Athens

Piso (28.1, 47): probably L. Calpurnius Piso Caesoninus, provincial governor of Macedonia

Pollux: see **Castor**

Polyxena (64.382): youngest daughter of Priam and Hecuba, the Trojan king and queen

Pompey (29.25): Gnaeus Pompeius Magnus, Pompey the Great

Pontic (4.8): adjective referring to the Black Sea

Porcius (47.1): unknown

Poseidon (64.3): Greek god of the sea, earthquakes, and horses, counterpart of the Roman **Neptune**

Postumia (27.4): unknown

Postumius (67.46): unknown

Procne (65.12): mythological figure who killed her son **Itys** to take revenge on her husband for raping her sister

Prometheus (64.310): a Titan, trickster god credited with giving human beings the gift of fire

Protesilaus (68.73): husband of **Laodamia**, killed at **Troy**

Quintia (82.1, 86): unknown, perhaps the sister of **Quintius**

Quintilia (96.1): probably the wife of M. **Licinius** Macer **Calvus**

Quintius (82.1, 100): unknown, perhaps the brother of **Quintia**

Ravidus (40.1): unknown

Rhesus (58b.4): a **Thracian** king who fought with the Trojans against the Greeks in Homer's *Iliad*

Rhoetean (65.8): adjective referring to **Troy**

Rufa (59.1): unknown

Rufulus (59.2): unknown

Rufus: (69.1, 77): perhaps M. Caelius Rufus; see **Caelius**

Sabine (39.11): adjective referring to an ancient region of Italy encompassing the central Apennines and Latium north of the Anio River

Sappho (51): sixth-century BC Greek lyric poet

Sappho's Muse (35.14): perhaps the goddess **Aphrodite** or poetry itself

Saturnalia (14.14): the Roman holiday falling nearest the winter solstice

Scamander (64.370): a river at **Troy**

Scylla (60.1): a mythological monster

Scythian (11.5): adjective referring to a region to the north and east of what is now western Europe

Septimius (45.1): unknown

Serapis (10.24): an Egyptian god whose cult gained popularity in Rome during Catullus' lifetime

Sestius (44.8): Publius Sestius, a well-known political figure in Catullus' time

Sileni (64.271): satyr-like worshippers of **Bacchus**/Dionysus

Sirmio (31.1): a peninsula at the southern end of Lake Garda near **Verona**

Socration (47.1): perhaps the Epicurean philosopher Philodemus

Stymphalian (68.109): an adjective referring to Stymphalos, modern Stymfalia, made famous by one of Heracles' twelve labors

Suffenus (14, 22): unknown

Sulla (14.8): unknown, perhaps a freedman of the famous Roman dictator Lucius Cornelius Sulla (Felix)

Syrtes (64.178): a reference to two bodies of water near North Africa

Talos (58b.1): a bronze giant crafted to be watchman on the island of Crete for the protection of either Minos or Europa

Taurian (64.130): adjective referring to the Taurus Mountains

Telemachus (61.192): son of Odysseus and **Penelope**

Tempe (64.44): a region of northern **Thessaly**

Temple of Jove (55.5): located on the Capitoline hill in Rome

Tethys (64.36, 66): a Titan, sister and wife of **Ocean** and goddess of the sea

Teucrian (64.357): adjective referring to the people of **Troy**

Thallus (25.1): unknown

Themis (68.147): a Titan, Greek goddess of law and order

Theseus (64.66): Athenian hero who slew the **Minotaur**

Thessaly (64.32): geographical region of what is now central Greece

Thetis (64.26, 34): Nereid, wife of Peleus, mother of Achilles

Thracian (4.7): adjective referring to Thrace, a region adjacent to **Marmara** on the Black Sea

Tiburtine (39.12): adjective referring to an ancient region of Italy around modern Tivoli in Lazio

Torquatus (61.182): the child imagined as the offspring of **Junia** and **Manlius**

Transpadane (39.14): adjective referring to a region north of the Po River

Trivia (34.14): Roman goddess of the crossroads, moon, and death, counterpart of the Greek Hecate

Troy (64.359, 68): the site of the Trojan War in what is now north-western Turkey

Urion (36.12): a city in Apulia

Varus: (10.1, 22): perhaps the lawyer Alfenus Varus or Quintilius Varus

Vatinius: (14.1, 52, 53): probably the politician P. Vatinius

Venus (3.1, 36, 45, 68): mother of Aeneas, Roman goddess of love and desire and counterpart of the Greek **Aphrodite**

Veranius (9.1, 12, 28, 47): unknown

Verona (17.1, 35, 67, 68, 100): the Italian city, birthplace of Catullus

Vesper (62.3): the evening star, Roman counterpart of the Greek Hesperus

Vibennius (33.1): unknown

Victus (98.1): unknown

Virgo (66.64): the constellation

Volusius (36.1, 95ab): unknown

Zephyr/Zephyrus (46.1, 66): the mythological name of the west wind, sometimes conflated with **Pegasus**

Zeus (34.6, 64): Greek sky god and king of the Greek pantheon, counterpart of the Roman **Jupiter/Jove**

Zmyrna (95ab.2): the name of **Cinna's** epyllion and the name of a mythological character who fell in love with her own father, Cinyras